THE
RE
GENERATION

Sowing Seeds for a Future of Reimagination,
Reconnection, and Regeneration

JACK ULDRICH & CAMILLE KOLLES

FC

**FAST
COMPANY**
Press

Fast Company Press
New York, New York
www.fastcompanypress.com

This work is being published under the Fast Company Press imprint
by an exclusive arrangement with *Fast Company*. *Fast Company* and the
Fast Company logo are registered trademarks of Mansueto Ventures,
LLC. The Fast Company Press logo is a wholly owned trademark of
Mansueto Ventures, LLC.

Distributed by River Grove Books

Design and composition by Greenleaf Book Group
Cover design by Greenleaf Book Group and Mimi Bark
Cover images used under license from @Shutterstock.com/tai11

Publisher's Cataloging-in-Publication data is available.

Hardcover ISBN: 978-1-63908-015-1

Paperback ISBN: 978-1-63908-016-8

eBook ISBN: 978-1-63908-017-5

First Edition

To Cindy, for reuniting our hearts,
reimagining the future together, and reconnecting us
to the things that matter most in life.
—Jack

To those working on the transformative edges of
integrating business, heart, and spirit, with gratitude
for advancing the known capacities of the human
spirit and illuminating its goodness.
—Camille

"Out of this darkness a new world can arise, not to be constructed by our minds so much as emerge from our dreams. Even though we cannot see clearly how it's going to turn out, we are still called to let the future into our imaginations. We will never be able to build what we have not first cherished in our hearts."

—JOANNA MACY

CONTENTS

THE RISE OF
GENERATION RE

"We are creating the future every day
by what we choose to do."

—MARGARET WHEATLEY

The world is changing. Old ways are dying, and a new world is being born. It's clear existing social and economic practices no longer produce the outcomes they once did, and stepping into this breach are untold numbers of creators implementing powerful new visions for a better world.

Many have been toiling to transform the world of business for decades. Some have embraced the ideals of conscious capitalism; others have dedicated their lives as social entrepreneurs seeking to solve social and environmental issues through business. Businesses have incorporated or reincorporated as public benefit corporations, including one or more public benefits right into their mission, while other businesses are rising to meet the standards of B Corp certification. Still other businesses and individuals are turning to impact investing, seeking to create significant value for investors and society as a whole. These are but a few of the many ways that attention to human values is emerging as vital to the future of business—and, frankly, the future of humanity.

Together, these individuals, businesses, and organizations are laying the foundations of a better, bolder, and more beautiful world. We call this collective human energy and those who embrace it *Generation Re*. This is a generation defined not by age but by ethos—an ethos of regeneration, rooted in the reunion of heart, spirit, and mind.

The ethos of Generation Re is consistent with aspirations to integrate the inner world of heart and spirit with the outer world of work and service. It represents a long-awaited reunion of the outer world with what is essential to the human spirit: the health of our mind, spirit, and physical body; considerations of love, compassion, forgiveness, empathy, and benevolence; and awareness of our interconnectedness to one another and the planet.

Recognizing business as a key shaper of society, Generation Re takes seriously the responsibility and power inherent in business to create a better world for all people. Moving beyond dominant paradigms of business as usual, Generation Re shifts into a new gear of daily intention that prioritizes and supports the spark of human connection and our deep need for making meaning and gives voice to the needs of our ailing planet. Members of Generation Re are living and working their way into an evolutionary paradigm shift—a shift in attention and intention from a primary value of *doing* to a primary value of *being*. Generation Re triumphs over the human tendency toward apathy, complacency, fear, or an attitude of "we've always done it this way" and is reinvigorating the human spirit as an active, uncompromising force for good in the world.

Five core themes are present in members of Generation Re:

- Reuniting minds, hearts, and spirits

- Reimagining business, capitalism, and the world anew

- Reexamining long-held assumptions, ineffective habits, and outdated beliefs

- Reframing old problems in creative new ways

- Redesigning for greater connection, in service to matters of ultimate concern for the health of one another and the planet

These *Re* aspirations, intentions, and skill sets create an overall spirit of regeneration, which is nudging us in the direction of a healthier, more inclusive, and more holistic world—and future. As Ernest Hemingway once wrote of another life-altering change, it happens "gradually, then suddenly." This transition from a primary focus on profit toward the integration of profit with larger arcs of meaning has been happening gradually, but now, it is poised to occur suddenly.

WHY BUSINESS?

"Organizations are not machines incessantly in need of repair, but instead are mysteries and miracles of human relatedness; they are living systems, webs of infinite strength and limitless human imagination."

—COOPERRIDER & SRIVASTVA

Business is a central locus of power in the world. The business ecosystem affects nearly every aspect of our lives, from birth to death and everything in between. Because of its pervasiveness, business has within it the power to positively affect and potentially transform our experience of everyday living. It has the power to either support or diminish the values we hold and cherish most deeply and the capacity to quite literally make or break the human spirit. In these ways, business holds one of the greatest keys to large-scale positive transformation.

We invite you to keep an open mind and an open heart about the great possibilities inherent in every aspect of the business ecosystem as we document how a number of businesses—both small and large—as well as individual business leaders, entrepreneurs, and social innovators, are rehumanizing business. We will introduce concepts that may seem incongruent with business. That's the point. We want to help build a bridge to a new way of thinking and being that is not only possible but also necessary for a thriving future, in which every business decision is based on larger human meaning and purpose.

For too long, business has operated as if it is a separate world from our personal life. As a result, this so-called outer world of business has been separated from the values we hold most deeply in our inner lives—love, compassion, empathy, and other qualities arising from the heart and spirit.

This is not just a fluffy fairy tale for wishful thinkers. Meaning and purpose in daily work are being demanded by younger generations. Humans' conscious awareness has evolved to the point where many of us no longer wish to live a life divided between outer work and the values most cherished in the human heart.

To this end, we invite you to open your heart and mind to

the monumental task of reuniting what never should have been separated in the first place—mind and heart, the material and the spiritual, humans and nature. We also invite you into the vital and energizing space of reimagining the future, and we will explore the role of reexamining our assumptions, habits, biases, and beliefs, as well as how Generation Re is employing this skill to great effect. We discuss the important work of reframing and of helping others see that creating deep change toward a better future is not something to be feared or attacked but, rather, an opportunity to be embraced. Once they have been embraced, the challenging work of redesigning a radically more beautiful future lies ahead. Finally, we'll illustrate how redesigning for interconnection can bring us closer to ourselves, our community, future generations, and the planet.

METAPHORS, STORIES, AND BUILDING SKILLS

"A map of the world that does not include Utopia is not worth even glancing at."

—OSCAR WILDE

At times, our discussion may resemble a grab bag of ideas ranging in nature from the purely practical to the audaciously aspirational. This range is intentional, in hopes of laying down steps that contribute to an increasingly traversed pathway of navigation between business and the heart. It is offered with gratitude to members of Generation Re for lighting up the world with possibility and illuminating multiple points of entry from which to join in their efforts and ethos.

No one has a map to this unknown world of the future, but leaders are called to boldly and courageously proceed into the future, for which few answers presently exist. Therefore, we will rely on metaphors, stories, quotes, poetry, and suggested insights for building skills in the hopes of inspiring you to take an active role in this emerging future.

The idea of using metaphors as maps is actually an ancient idea. Prior to the creation of the world's first navigational maps and atlases, maps did exist, but they did not serve the same function and purpose as maps do today. Rather than navigational, they were a medium designed to help people understand their place in the world by using history, myth, anthropology, scripture, and spirituality.

The T-O map (*orbis terrarum*) in figure 0.1 is one of the world's earliest known maps. The T represents the waters separating the then known continents of the world—Asia, Europe, and Africa—while the O encircling the entire image reflects the idea during this period that the world was surrounded by water.

Figure 0.1. The T-O map.

Unlike modern maps, the T-O map was less concerned with accurately measuring the physical world and more concerned with helping people find their place in a world of shared meaning. In this sense, the map was telling people a story. We seek to do the same: We profile only a small fraction of the many extraordinary individuals, businesses, organizations, and institutions operating from a *Re ethos*, but through them, we attempt to tell a story and a vision of greater meaning.

And just as the ancient T-O map was arguably more ambitious in its intentions than a navigational map, we aim in this book to animate a new, larger story, full of possibility, that inspires, galvanizes, and equips readers to find their own way to join the ethos of those who are birthing a regenerative future.

IMAGINAL CELLS

"There is another world but it is in this one."

—W. B. YEATS

How do you begin to reimagine and redesign a regenerative world? Let's begin by considering the humble caterpillar. Caterpillars go through metamorphosis to become butterflies, but the more granular process of metamorphosis serves as a wonderful metaphor for incubating our collective future.

Inside every caterpillar is something known as *imaginal cells*, which can be thought of as the seeds of future potential. The cells contain the blueprint of the butterfly, as well as the source code for future regeneration.

The imaginal cells initially operate independently, as single-cell organisms and, in the beginning, are perceived as a threat by the caterpillar. They are attacked by its immune system. At this stage, it appears as though the caterpillar will consume itself and turn into organic ooze.

But this isn't what happens. The imaginal cells persist, grow, multiply, and begin communicating with one another. This communication establishes the beginning of a network that serves to draw new cells into the transformative process. This creates a positive feedback loop that forms an even larger, stronger, more cooperative network and, in turn, draws in ever more cells.

A tipping point soon occurs, and out of this ooze emerges a beautiful butterfly—a creature utterly unlike the caterpillar. Although the transformation is miraculous in and of itself, even more astonishing is this: All of the components of the butterfly were always present in the caterpillar. They just needed to be shown that a different possibility existed.

We encourage you to consider the individuals, businesses, corporations, and organizations profiled in the book as analogous to the original imaginal cells in a caterpillar. Often operating under the radar, they are nonetheless incubating, creating, and fostering blueprints for conducting business in ways that support the needs of the human spirit, laying the foundation for a radically more beautiful future.

We share their blueprints in the form of stories, with the hope that you will be drawn into the ethos of this growing network and will be inspired—with a united heart and mind—to join in hastening the transformations.

SHIFTS IN WORLDVIEW

Copernicus ushered in a paradigm shift of epic proportions by altering humankind's belief that Earth was at the center of the universe. This Copernican revolution shook powerful institutions in demonstrating that long-held assumptions could be inaccurate.

Throughout this book, members of Generation Re demonstrate how a spirit dedicated to higher ideals can overturn stubborn, long-held beliefs no longer useful and can reconnect business to the human ideals that make life worth living. Renewing your dedication to higher ideals involves altering your perception of what's possible and questioning often unconscious assumptions, including ideas about reality itself.

As you contemplate how these descriptions of Generation Re fit into your own mental framework, take a look at the card in figure 0.2. At first glance, the visual might not strike you as unusual but, after a short time, it should become evident that the card does not abide by traditional rules: It is a black diamond.

Figure 0.2. The six of diamonds.

Perhaps you did not immediately pick up on this odd discrepancy because you easily slotted the visual into an old belief system. That is, you either thought it was a black club or spade without noticing it was a diamond, or you thought it was a spade without noticing it was the wrong color. Likewise, it may be easy to place Generation Re into a pre-existing category, but we suggest it may be more fruitful to see its ethos as a powerful collection of emerging human energies seeking to rejoin long-separated divisions of heart and mind—a reunion that will, in time, overturn current thinking that no longer serves humanity.

THE INVITATION

"As idiotic as optimism may seem
it has a weird way of paying off."

—MICHAEL LEWIS

As you read, we invite you to consider your own insights in integrating factors related to business decision-making and matters that are essential to the human spirit. Perhaps you are already Re-ing and may discover in reading the profiles an even greater fearlessness and enthusiasm within yourself for forging new ground. Perhaps you have considered your own sense of dividedness and will find comfort in knowing there's a movement afoot that seeks to reunite this fragmentation. Perhaps you know in your heart that business has tremendous power to transform the world if it can only reach more deeply into the wellsprings of hopes, dreams, and ideals that nourish every living thing. Whatever the case, we hope you uncover aspirations that embolden you to join in the ethos of Generation Re.

As fellow travelers, we see our role as *permissionaries*, granting the reader permission to transcend cynicism and the way things have always been done. We are tasked with encouraging you to follow a deeper calling toward an integration of head and heart. The biggest mistake cynics and pessimists make is that they mistake their isms for realism. The only people who have created a better future are those who believed they could.

We will also make the argument that individuals and businesses that don't reimagine, reconnect, and renew themselves, their businesses, their communities, and the planet will not only miss a once-in-a-lifetime opportunity to reform the world, but they may also find themselves out of business.

Why? First, companies hewing to business as usual won't be able to attract the type of creative, compassionate, empathetic, imaginative, and wise employees who are capable of bringing this new regenerative future into existence. If this higher purpose isn't already baked into your organization's vision and mission, you are unlikely to find Generation Re recruits. Second, many businesses will be rendered obsolete because forward-looking customers embracing the ethos of Generation Re won't want to do business with those who aren't helping create the type of future the customer desires. And finally, current business-as-usual practices are not compatible with the natural laws of a regenerative organism.

KOKORO: THE CONVERGENCE OF MIND, HEART, AND SPIRIT

"The institutions and leaders who understand the power of our spiritset and the infinite potential that it offers will be the ones to survive and flourish in increasingly challenging times."

—JOHN HAGEL, former cochair,
Deloitte's Center for the Edge

Generation Re possesses a characteristic that is difficult to name because no phrase in English adequately captures its holistic nature. John Hagel, cochair of Deloitte's Center for the Edge, has written about mindset, heartset, and spiritset, which hint at it. But the word that comes closest is the Japanese *kokoro*, which refers to a union of mind, heart, and spirit.

In the Western worldview, people tend to speak of each of these things separately and, sometimes, even collectively (as in "the mind and the heart and the spirit") but not as an integrated whole. The beauty of kokoro is that it dispenses with the word *and*, potentially providing an opening for business leaders and others to wrestle with the seemingly disparate concerns of these three realms. But the barriers between these three realms are more tenuous than we have been led to believe, and their effective dismantling is key to freeing the world of business to grow to its greatest potential.

It is a cliché to say that you must change yourself before you can change others, much less change the future, but there is great truth to this, and for this reason we begin with the notion of reuniting within ourselves.

Chapter 1

REUNITE

*"At the deepest level of the human heart
there is no simple singular self."*

—JOHN O'DONOHUE

The William Blake painting *Newton* (figure 1.1) may seem an unusual place to begin a book aimed at a business audience, but the painting serves as a powerful metaphor for the topic of reunion. It hints at what must be rejoined if the future is to be regenerative.

The painting depicts the division of the human capacity for rational thinking from our essential connection to the natural world. This fundamentally flawed but persistent worldview of humans as separate from nature is also evident in the dualistic thinking that divides physical matter from the nonmaterial world of ideals and values. This division, underlying prevailing assumptions in industrialized society, cries out for reunion if we are to evolve from dependence on destructive ways of being into the fully thriving and regenerative world of tomorrow.

Figure 1.1 William Blake's Newton.

In the painting, Newton appears to be seated on the bottom of the ocean, crouched on a seabed, where he is drawing a geometrical design on a paper scroll with a compass. It depicts Blake's frustration with Newton's limited view, reflecting the idea that Newton, while studying one reality with a compass, is ignoring and isolating himself from another equally important reality. The other reality—the ocean—represents a more mysterious and mostly unseen world.

The image suggests that Newton's attention is limited to only those ideas that can be captured with data and the tools of science. This is reflective of a philosophical materialism, which, very simply defined, purports that only physical matter is real. It was Blake's belief that Newton was clipping the wings of nature, imagination, and all those things that make life rich and meaningful.

Over time, the idea that the only reality is that which can be measured became a foundation for today's dominant mindset and worldview. This worldview fails to give equal weight to the poetic, spiritual, meaning-making center of human nature, and it has a firm grip on today's business world. As Blake astutely observed, it is dangerously limiting in outlook.

This material-centric mindset has unquestionably brought about extraordinary industrial and technological progress and ushered untold numbers of people out of extreme poverty. But, divided as it is from the ideals of the human spirit and our inter-connected nature, it has also brought the world to the brink of environmental and ecological disaster while eroding our ability to find meaning and genuine fulfillment in our daily lives.

If business is to drive the change that the world needs, it is imperative that business leaders begin seeing the whole picture once again. We must work to reunite the material with the spiritual.

This notion of the need to shift our worldview to reunite matter and spirit, the seen with the unseen, the known with the unknown, and the measurable with unmeasurable isn't new. In the Amazon rainforest, an ancient prophecy of the eagle and condor warns of the dangers of this divided path and foretells of the renaissance that awaits in the paths' convergence.

According to the legend, 500 years ago human society took two divergent paths, the path of the eagle and that of the condor. The former represents the peoples of the northern hemisphere and is associated with the rational, the masculine, and technological and scientific knowledge. The condor path is associated with the heart, the intuitive, the feminine, and a connection with nature. The prophecy says that the future of the world depends on the two coming together to reach a new, heightened level of global consciousness. The two birds soaring together in the sky as equals is said to represent the enlightenment of humanity.

Before we can play a role in either bringing the prophecy to fruition or playing a meaningful role in this evolution, we must first look inward.

AN IRISH MONK UNLEARNS

"Yesterday I was clever so I wanted to change the world.
Today I am wise so I am changing myself."

—RUMI

A few years ago, there was a popular story making the rounds on the internet. It was questionably attributed to an Irish monk in the eleventh century, but whatever the source, it serves as another useful metaphor. According to the story, the monk said,

> *When I was a young man, I wanted to change the world. I found it was difficult to change the world so I tried to change my country. When I realized I couldn't change my country, I focused on changing my community. I then realized I couldn't change my community and, as I grew into middle age, I worked on changing my family.*
>
> *Now, as an old man, I realize the only thing I can change is myself. In changing myself, however, I have come to realize I can change my family and, by changing my family I can change my community, and by changing my community I realize I can change the world.*

Countless wisdom traditions guide us to aspire to change the world by first changing ourselves. In this spirit, let's begin by examining a reunion of mind and heart.

REUNITING MIND AND HEART

"The heart has its reasons of which reason knows nothing."
—BLAISE PASCAL

Before you continue reading, place your right hand on your heart, take a deep breath in, and press your hand down on your heart. With each breath, repeat the gentle motion, and imagine, with each pump, a deeper imprint being made on your heart.

This exercise might seem softhearted and to have no place in today's fast-paced, ever-changing, hypercompetitive business arena, but the opposite is the case. Managers and leaders have been trained and conditioned so thoroughly that they view as an almost unchallenged assumption that business and matters of the heart are separate and that the latter are inappropriate to bring into the workplace. How often have you heard it said that "you can't let your heart rule your head"? Clearly, this needs reconsideration.

Recall the Japanese concept of kokoro introduced earlier that integrates the meanings of heart, mind, and spirit. Similarly, the Chinese word *xin* captures this weaving together of heart, mind, feeling, intention, and essence. In Buddhism, the Pali or Sanskrit word *citta* has multiple meanings, one of which relays a similar sense of an awakened and combined heart–mind. The English language possesses no comparable words, but its speakers strive to reach this integrated meaning indirectly.

Consider, for a moment, all the ways we use the word *heart*. Have you ever had a heart-to-heart talk, put your heart into something, opened your heart to someone, had your heart in the right place, felt young at heart, or had your heart broken? Have you ever taken heart, followed your heart, or touched someone's heart?

"Some things don't matter much. Like the color of a house. How big is that in the overall scheme of life? But lifting a person's heart— now that matters. The whole problem with people is that they know what matters, but they don't choose it. The hardest thing on Earth is choosing what matters."

—SUE MONK KIDD

What about meeting someone who was all heart, a bleeding heart, or had a tender heart or a heart of gold? Have you ever lost heart, had a change of heart, or acted from the bottom of your heart? Have you ever poured your heart out to someone, known someone who wore their heart on their sleeve, or had a boss who had your best interests at heart? Have you ever had a heavy heart, had your heart go to someone, or found it in your heart to forgive someone? Have you ever expressed a heartfelt emotion, or engaged in a task that did your heart some good? Such metaphors pervade our daily lives, and the present times are calling us to deeply integrate the mind with that other wellspring of human capacity—the heart.

According to the HeartMath Institute, a heart cell's electrical output is exceptional: Each heartbeat produces two and a half watts of electrical energy. This is 40 to 60 times that of brain waves and is enough to power a small light bulb. This energy also creates an electromagnetic field that radiates out 12–15 feet from the human body.[1]

FROM DOING TO BEING

"Your heart knows the way. Run in that direction."

—RUMI

One racing heart[2] and a single extra heartbeat[3] may appear a weak foundation on which to stake a claim that business is not just an extraordinary force for revolutionary change but could also lead to an evolutionary shift in consciousness. However, two exemplars of Generation Re, by following their hearts, are representative of the widening embrace of the Re ethos and are changing business and making strides in transforming their fields of work.

The OBO Movement

Generation Re recognizes the degree to which a dominant worldview in business today—the idea that something only matters if it can be measured—has fostered a disconnection between human flourishing and economic models.

An exemplar of this notion is Dev Tandon, a CEO, entrepreneur, and former McKinsey consultant who is intent on rehumanizing business. He seeks a rebirth of business as we know it.

Something is terribly wrong in the world of business. In spite of decades of economic growth and technological advancement, hundreds of millions of people continue to be deprived of their basic needs while the planet is being pushed beyond its limits due to the excesses of businesses. And in the midst of this advancement and productivity, many are challenged to find a sense of meaning.

Now, imagine a world in which business, one of the largest levers for societal change, not only supports employees financially but also helps them flourish emotionally, physically, and spiritually.

To many people, this seems unimaginable. Dev Tandon is not one of those people. After a profound epiphany on a flight from California to Mexico, he imagined a different way of doing business, a way of rehumanizing business.

After first thinking, *Who am I to think I can change business and change the world?* Tandon decided instead to "follow his racing heart." After days of brainstorming, he created what he calls the OBO movement. OBO stands for "or best offer," and it is based on the radical idea that a business's true mission is to help awaken its employees.

For too long, business has valued money over human connection, and Tandon realized that, by focusing on connection, everyone—rich and poor—could have more. For Tandon, OBO is not a new way of doing business; it is a new way of being.

The initial step in the OBO premise is helping employees reflect on and find their life's purpose. In doing so, Tandon believes these awakening employees (he prefers the term *participants*) will change the company, and, in time, their inner change will manifest itself outward and positively change suppliers, customers, communities, and—ultimately—the world.

Without getting deeper into the OBO method (for this, read Tandon's excellent book, *The OBO Premise: A Bold Vision for Business*), it is important to understand that he began by embracing the idea that the only way to change the world was by changing himself first.

A student of meditation, Tandon came to adopt what he calls the threefold path: right volition, right action, and right outcome. In his own words, the concept is simple but not easy. If a person has the right volition, which can be thought of as the right intention or virtue—love, compassion, trust, transparency, inclusion, balance, integrity—and then follows that volition with right action, the outcome, whatever it is, will be the right outcome.

True leaders, when they look into their hearts, understand that they did not come into this world to lead based on fear. They came here to act on higher principles and on behalf of a more noble purpose.

In this regard, it may be helpful to recall the metaphor of the imaginal cells. In the beginning, the imaginal cells are attacked by the host's immune system because they are perceived as a threat. The attacks don't prevent the transformation; they merely delay it. In a similar way, the forces of business as usual may attack the early imaginal cells of Generation Re. But this is no reason to give up on an opportunity to manifest your visions for a better world. You need only be aware of the natural forces that push back against new ideas.

Perhaps you are skeptical of the possibility of widespread systemic change based on engaging and awakening your heart and the hearts of your employees.

First, it may be difficult to comprehend how a business can profitably sustain itself and, at the same time, meet the physical, emotional, and spiritual needs of its employees. This assumption needs to be challenged. Dev Tandon himself is operating his new business on this premise, and, on his website, he lists a growing number of other businesses that are operating in this same manner. They include Natura, a multibillion-dollar Brazilian conglomerate, which begins its hiring process by creating space to talk about purpose and meaning. A sample of the questions the company asks its employees includes "What is each person's purpose in life that is greater than their own existence?" and "What would allow them to die with a sense of integrity that their life was worth living?"[4]

Second, you might question the scalability of such a business model, given the still-prevailing model that prioritizes profit at the expense of other values essential for a balanced life. The growing number of companies embracing consciousness capitalism and stakeholder capitalism or becoming either public benefits corporations or certified B Corporations suggests that businesses' singular focus on monetary profits alone is diminishing. Accelerating this trend is the fact that ever more employees are clamoring to work at companies with aspirations that transcend mere profit.

Third, you might persist in thinking that the vast majority

of today's customers only care about price and convenience and that it is unreasonable to expect a business to meet the financial, physical, emotional, and spiritual needs of its employees while also remaining competitive. At a surface level, this thinking may appear logical, but on closer examination, it doesn't stand up to scrutiny.

A useful way to think about how this could possibly work is to consider company actions in terms of energy input. The prevailing business model uses advertising, marketing, social media, price, and convenience to hook customers. All of these hooks require an exertion of energy to reel the customer in. Contrast this with a relationship based on the right volition of love, truth, or compassion. These invisible forces are attractors as well, and businesses that weave these qualities of the heart into their operations move into a new realm of energy exchange that is fundamentally more real than the superficial hooks. We can now begin to see how integrating these qualities is not counter to profit but inclusive of it. It represents the next necessary evolutionary stage of business.

This integration of business and the heart need not be a far-fetched dream. Hastened by your participation in the ethos of Generation Re, it can become the prevailing wisdom. Integral philosopher Ken Wilber has speculated that an "integral tipping point" is achieved when "10 percent of the population grows into a new structure of meaning-making." At this percentage, Wilbur says, "a whole new society is able to rewrite its public rules based on that structure."[5] Supporting this speculation is a 2011 study by scientists at the Rensselaer Polytechnic Institute, who found that "when just 10 percent of a population holds an unshakeable belief, their belief will be adopted by the majority."[6]

If reservations about the practicality of a reunion of heart and mind in business persist in your mind, consider this: Is cynicism really more useful than hope? Is it really that impractical to have more confidence in love and compassion than cold-hearted competition? As Bertrand Russell, the British polymath and philosopher said, "The reasonable man adapts himself to the world; the unreasonable one persists in trying to adapt the world to himself. Therefore, all progress depends on the unreasonable man." You are encouraged to stay open to unreasonable propositions.

All Square restaurant

> *"The longest journey you'll ever take is*
> *from your head to your heart."*
> —SIOUX SAYING

Throughout her life, Emily Hunt Turner has worn her heart on her sleeve. But after a few years of trying to use her position as a federal attorney to help people locate stable housing, she grew frustrated. Federal law still allows those who have been incarcerated to be denied housing. This frustration, during a period of increasing awareness of other institutionalized bias, led to a turning point in her heart and spirit. One day, Hunt Turner woke up with an "extra heartbeat" and a burning desire to start a business that would invest in formerly incarcerated citizens to address systemic racism and the widespread exclusion of those with prison records.

With little more than a dream, Hunt Turner founded All Square, a restaurant that employs only formerly incarcerated individuals. The name serves two purposes. First, it denotes that the purpose of her restaurant is to honor the idea that formerly incarcerated individuals have paid their debts to society and are, therefore, all square in the eyes of society. The name also highlights that the restaurant features square, craft grilled cheese sandwiches in a metaphorical reference to its purpose.

A former civil rights attorney who started a restaurant as a civil rights social enterprise may seem another unlikely example for a business book. But to understand the growing influence of Generation Re, it is important to understand how they are listening to their hearts and leveraging business in innovative and unconventional ways.

All Square hints at the future of business capacity by demonstrating that a business itself can be a mechanism for integrating and addressing deep community needs. While the enterprise is a nonprofit that includes an entrepreneurial fellowship program, the restaurant earns revenue as its employees gain critical life skills.

In addition to hiring only formerly incarcerated individuals (who Hunt Turner refers to as "justice impacted") and providing them a living wage, her enterprise also pays them to attend the Dream Lab for 10 hours every week. The lab serves as a reentry program that offers people returning from prison a yearlong fellowship where they take classes in everything from law and entrepreneurship to personal finance, budgeting, resume writing, social media marketing, and soft skills training. There are even mental health and wellness services to meet the physical and emotional needs of the employees.

All Square's employees are gaining the skills to thrive. Although the enterprise only began in 2018, members of the first fellowship cohort have gone on to become paralegals, law school students, wedding boutique owners, and food truck operators.

Beyond meeting important individual needs, All Square also serves as a place where people with perceived differences—such as those affected by mass incarceration and their neighbors—can come together to break bread. Hunt Turner is reconnecting justice-impacted individuals to their community and, in turn, helping the community to understand that these individuals deserve to be judged on their merit and not their mistakes.

Before the restaurant even opened, the community was resonating with Hunt Turner's plans. After she was denied a traditional business loan by the bank, the community came together and invested $60,000 through a Kickstarter campaign and tens of thousands of dollars in additional supporting memberships.[7]

Since that time, word of mouth, a quality product, favorable press (including her social enterprise being named one of the world's 100 greatest places in 2019 by *Time* magazine), and a heart-centered mission have allowed her business to prosper. By listening to that extra heartbeat, Hunt Turner is one step closer to her broader mission: to disrupt the way society perceives formerly incarcerated individuals.

At a broader and deeper level, All Square points to a regenerative future because Hunt Turner's employees can not only find employment, get credit, and rent an apartment, but they are also able, once again, to dream about building a constructive future for themselves and their families. For too long, those who were incarcerated have lived with a poverty of dreams precisely because they couldn't get all square after serving their time.

THE POWER OF AMPLIFICATION

This idea of dreaming might sound soft and unbusinesslike, but businesses such as Hunt Turner's—more so than traditional, exclusively profit-focused businesses—are transforming the world. The famous adage that "a butterfly flapping its wings can unleash a hurricane on the other side of the world" seems apropos here. The butterfly effect has been verified by chaos theorists, who have demonstrated that any action, no matter how small, has the potential, through the power of amplification, to change the world.

Businesses such as Hunt Turner's and Tandon's have a greater chance of changing the world because their mission and the work resonate at the level of the human heart. This heart resonance, together with the feeling of interconnection it fosters, activates the positive emotions of others, who provide word-of-mouth support and economic patronage.

An easy way to understand the power of amplification is to consider cases where people voluntarily pay it forward. In Florida, 378 consecutive patrons at a Starbucks purchased the order for the person behind them. In 2020, in an economically depressed region of northern Minnesota, 914 patrons paid it forward at a local Dairy Queen over the course of 2.5 days.[8]

Traditional economic theory would suggest that such trends would never begin, because the first person would simply accept the kind act and not reciprocate. Undoubtedly, this happens sometimes, but, as these two cases demonstrate, the human spirit also loves to give.

Chad Houser is another big-hearted individual who has united his culinary passion with social justice by leaving his prestigious positions as an award-winning chef in Dallas to start Cafe Momentum, a restaurant designed to break the cycle of violence, crime, and incarceration by helping youth learn new life skills.

Houser's restaurant, which is operated entirely by former incarcerated youth, has reduced recidivism among its employees threefold while becoming the third-highest-rated restaurant in Dallas. Moreover, Houser is changing the narrative and reversing the stereotype for these youth. One longtime veteran juvenile detention officer even publicly admitted that he was wrong after seeing—and tasting—what these young people could accomplish.

Within the coming years, Houser, who is not afraid to acknowledge and openly speak of his unconditional love for his kids, plans to scale Cafe Momentum to 30 cities and reshape how people think about juvenile justice.

You might place Tandon, Hunt Turner, or Houser into a special category of people where you don't belong, but think again. They have simply decided to meet their aspirations head-on and to manifest them in the world. Fortunately, this courage and its grounding in a reunion of inner and outer lives can be cultivated and fostered.

SKILLS AND INSIGHTS FOR REUNITING

"We are not human beings having a spiritual experience. We are spiritual beings having a human experience."

—PIERRE TEILHARD DE CHARDIN

Since the 1960s, the Gallup organization has been measuring the frequency of mystical experiences in the United States. In a recent poll, 84 percent of the respondents indicated that they had had at least one experience in which they "went beyond their ordinary self and felt connected to something greater than themselves." In the same survey, a follow-up question revealed that 75 percent of the respondents agreed there was a social taboo against speaking in public about such experiences.[9]

Figure 1.2. The Storyteller *is an Inuit stone carving. The open eye looks outward, seeing the world of material reality. The closed eye looks inward, focusing on the inner world of dreams and the imagination.*

In other words, a solid majority of Americans have had a profound connection to some form of the infinite, but most people didn't feel comfortable speaking about these meaningful experiences. At a personal level, this discrepancy speaks to the disconnection between peoples' minds, hearts, and spirits. At a broader level, it also helps explain the persistent and profoundly erroneous separation of matters of the spirit from action in the business world. Because such experiences of the infinite are more commonly shared than perhaps first assumed, imagine the depth of communication and connection that could open up between us if we each were willing to broach this topic with one another.

To facilitate more fluid navigation between our outer work in the world of business and the inner dimensions of heart and spirit, between the seen and unseen worlds, consider the following as potentially useful insights for building such skills.

Keep the end in mind

> *"The passport to living is to imagine yourself in the grave."*
>
> —ANTHONY DE MELLO

"I know we're going to die, but some of us are going to do something about it." The meaning of the first part of this statement is obvious. All of us know that we are going to die at some point. What makes the statement particularly stirring is that it was uttered by Thomas Burnett, a passenger on United Flight 93 on September 11, 2001. Burnett helped steer a plane into the Pennsylvania countryside and prevented it from being used as a weapon to inflict even more horrific damage on an unsuspecting public than the planes that had just crashed into the Twin Towers in New York.

Fortunately, few of us will ever be confronted with our own mortality in such a stark, vivid, and terrifying manner. But if we wish to reunite with the things that matter the most in our lives, contemplating our death well before it seems imminent can be a powerful tool for personal development. The art of living is enriched by thinking about death.

Figure 1.3. Frida Kahlo's Thinking about Death.

"Come to terms with death.
Thereafter, anything is possible."

—ALBERT CAMUS

Confronting death can be profound in many ways. For example, certain activities, unconventional though they may be, can shift your perspective by reminding you of what really matters. You may wish to try the following ideas.

Attend a funeral at least once a year, even if you do not know the deceased. Far from being a morbid task, the experience can change your life, especially if you listen closely to the eulogies. Almost universally, the themes expressed in these stories of a life commemorated have little to do with material success. Rather, most often the remembrances center on what uniquely lit up their spirit and how they showed kindness, generosity, and love. These are qualities that we all have access to in equal measure.

Draft your own eulogy. Focus on how and what you hope to be remembered for in this life. To keep it real for yourself, it may be useful to consider these questions: Are the decisions you're making today (at work and otherwise) the same as those you would make from an end-of-life perspective? Do your daily decisions reflect the greater wisdom you know you are capable of? Do you keep in mind what really matters? Are your personal practices in harmony with the natural world?

We all owe life a death. If you wish to deny this, it might be helpful to recall the Greek myth of Tithonus, who was gifted immortality by Zeus. In the end, he petitioned the gods for death so that his actions and his life would matter. The bottom line is this: If we shrink from our deaths, we shrink from our lives.

Move beyond a desire for certainty

> *"Certainty begets stagnation, but ambiguity*
> *pulls us deeper into life."*
>
> —JAMES HOLLIS, *What Matters Most*

What do you see in the picture in figure 1.4? Most people see either a rabbit or a duck. The picture is a simple, albeit clever, optical illusion, and it is relatively easy to see both figures once the other image has been pointed out.

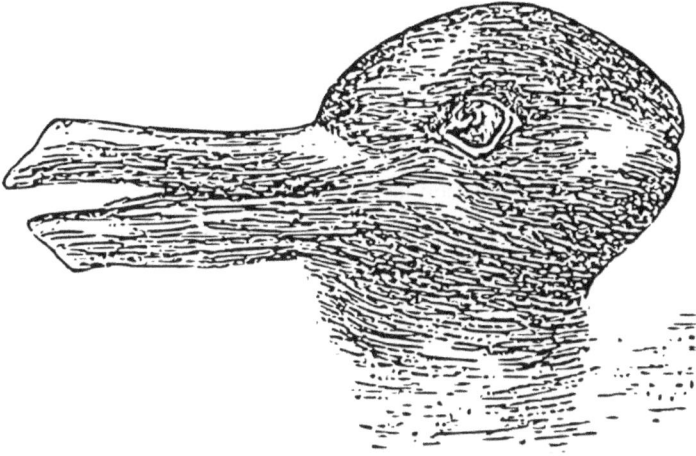

Figure 1.4. Can you see both a rabbit and a duck?

Doing the same with our minds—moving beyond binary, either/or thinking—is far more challenging. But if we can begin to move beyond our customary categories of thinking into the messier places of uncertainty, we can begin to integrate the lesser-known areas of our heart and spirit with a mind that clings to the usual frameworks of logic and personal opinion.

Voltaire once said that "doubt is an unpleasant condition, but certainty is absurd." In spite of the wisdom of this statement, many of us resort to rigid categorical thinking as a way to manage, minimize, and eliminate uncertainty.

The truth is that our lives are more uncertain than we acknowledge, and holding on too tightly to a desire for certainty has the undesirable effect of clouding our view and distorting our sense of reality. Relatedly, when we play to our penchant for reductionism, reducing complex phenomena to overly simplified explanations, we deprive ourselves of the immense potentialities of richer, more nuanced understandings that would naturally make more room for matters of the heart.

The following scenario offers a hint of how thinking in shades of gray can begin to open up a fuller spectrum of possibilities:

A stranger asks you for the best route between two well-known points in your community. Since you're familiar with the area, a route instantly springs to mind, and you provide the stranger with the answer. But a thorough examination of the situation will quickly reveal the limitations of this approach. The "best" route from the perspective of a busy person is the fastest route. For a retired person, the best route may be the most scenic. For a history enthusiast, the best may be the road with the most interesting past. For a walker, the best route could be that with the flattest terrain, and for an extreme athlete, it may be the most arduous route. A beginning driver might prefer the safest route, while an environmentalist, concerned about future generations, might desire the most environmentally friendly route.

If such a simple, straightforward question can be parsed so many ways, what of life's more complex questions? Perhaps we can make more room for matters of the heart by widening our lens of perception to include the messier areas of uncertainty.

"The moral measure of a culture is found in the degree
to which individuals and groups can tolerate ambiguity and
change and how open they can be to the otherness of others."

—JAMES HOLLIS, *Living an Examined Life*

Read poetry

*"It is difficult to get news from a poem, yet men die
miserably every day for lack of what is found there."*

—WILLIAM CARLOS WILLIAMS

There are a number of practical reasons for business leaders to read poetry. Poetry can sharpen your perceptiveness and foster empathy. It can speak the language of the heart, touching centers of feeling in ways that mere prose cannot. The quality of nuance in poetry can also assist us in navigating the complexity of today's rapidly changing world. Poetry can also assist in these uncertain times by gently inviting its readers to embrace paradox and ambiguity. As David Whyte says, "Poetry is able to hold the dark and the light together and not turn its face away from either."

Reading poetry can stimulate the imagination and spark creativity, essential traits for any business looking to innovate into the future. As Percy Shelley wrote, "Poets are the unacknowledged legislators of the world." That is to say, from a poet's integration of mind, heart, and spirit is imagined a higher order of things, which, when expressed and then absorbed into the wider consciousness, can form the basis of new elements of civil society.

*"Clothed in facts truth feels oppressed; in the garb
of poetry it moves easy and free."*

—TAGORE

The ability to lift the veil on the invisible world and to remind us of the existence of greater beauty and deeper meaning makes poetry a surprisingly useful tool for those who seek to better integrate business and matters of the heart. To paraphrase the previous Williams quote, you can get information from *The Wall Street Journal*, business books, and profit and loss statements, but poetry exposes deeper universal truths, gently nudging us to remember those immeasurable things that matter most in life.

Embrace paradox

> *"The test of a first-rate intelligence is the ability to hold two opposed ideas in mind at the same time and still retain the ability to function."*
>
> —F. SCOTT FITZGERALD

Wisdom traditions throughout history have revered the paradox—a statement that is seemingly contradictory or opposed to common sense but that is perhaps true. The ability to embrace paradox is a critical skill, because it allows us to comprehend how the most important things are often the most difficult to measure.

Niels Bohr, the Nobel Prize–winning physicist, once said, "The opposite of a true statement is a false statement; the opposite of a profound truth can be another profound truth. The poles of a paradox are like the poles of a battery: Hold them together, and they generate the energy of life; pull them apart, and the current stops flowing. When we separate any of the profound paired truths of our lives, both poles become lifeless spectres of themselves, and we become lifeless as well."[10] In short, Bohr was recognizing paradoxes as essential, because they connect us to the vibrancy of life.

WHAT WILL MATTER?

Michael Josephson

Ready or not, some day it will all come to an end.

There will be no more sunrises, no minutes, hours or days.

All the things you collected, whether treasured

or forgotten will pass to someone else.

Your wealth, fame and temporal power will shrivel to irrelevance.

It will not matter what you owned or what you were owed.

Your grudges, resentments, frustrations and jealousies will finally disappear.

So too, your hopes, ambitions, plans and to-do lists will expire.

The wins and losses that once seemed so important will fade away.

It won't matter where you came from

or what side of the tracks you lived on at the end.

It won't matter whether you were beautiful or brilliant.

Even your gender and skin color will be irrelevant.

So what will matter? How will the value of your days be measured?

What will matter is not what you bought

but what you built, not what you got but what you gave.

What will matter is not your success but your significance.

What will matter is not what you learned but what you taught.

What will matter is every act of integrity, compassion, courage, or sacrifice

that enriched, empowered or encouraged others to emulate your example.

What will matter is not your competence but your character.

What will matter is not how many people you knew,

but how many will feel a lasting loss when you're gone.

What will matter is not your memories but

the memories that live in those who loved you.

What will matter is how long you will be remembered, by whom and for what.

Living a life that matters doesn't happen by accident.

It's not a matter of circumstance but of choice.

Choose to live a life that matters.

Interestingly, science is catching up with wisdom traditions in discoveries that require holding two oppositional ideas. Quantum physics, for example, accepts the reality that a photon can be a particle and a wave at the same time. In the field of quantum computing, scientists have even leveraged a qubit's ability to simultaneously represent a zero and a one, a uniquely quantum phenomenon known as *superposition*, to manufacture mind-bogglingly powerful computers.

Figure 1.5. Waterfall *by M. C. Escher. Escher's classic perpetual motion machine offers a fun, paradoxical visual. The water appears to flow both up and down at the same time.*

The significance of holding two seemingly opposed ideas in mind at once can be felt when considering the following paradoxes:

- All people are the same. All people are different.

- Seeking only our own happiness is the surest way to remain unhappy.

- When we see others as strangers, we are estranged from ourselves.

- By seeing the contrast with others, we can awaken to our alikeness.

- We experience the world as separate and fragmented, but our underlying reality is one of wholeness.

As to this wholeness, Albert Einstein famously said, "A human being is a part of the whole called by us *universe*, a part limited in time and space. He experiences himself, his thoughts and feelings, as something separated from the rest, a kind of optical delusion of his consciousness." Martin Luther King alluded to much the same when he said, "Whatever affects one directly affects all indirectly. I can never be what I ought to be until you are what you ought to be. This is the interrelated structure of reality."

Challenge your worldview

> *"We see the world in terms of our theories."*
>
> —THOMAS KUHN

A worldview is the set of beliefs about fundamental aspects of reality that ground and influence your perception, thinking, knowledge, and action.[11] It is also defined as a collection of attitudes, values, stories, and expectations about the world around us, which inform our every thought and action.[12] Prior to Copernicus and Galileo, one aspect of worldview was the belief that Earth was at the center of the universe.

It can be challenging enough to encounter ideas about how the world works or to witness ways of perceiving that are new to you. Even more challenging is the task of weaving these new ideas into your deep-seated and complex worldview. And how much more challenging still it can be when the new seems to defy your experience of reality. For example, Earth does seem stable, and we see the sun move every day, as though it revolves around the planet.

But challenging your worldview is essential for progressing on the pathway toward integration of the heart and the mind. This pathway requires a hard look at your biases, assumptions, and habituations, which so often function to prematurely categorize.

Consider the six common assumptions below, worthy of being challenged.

- Business is one thing, and matters of the heart are separate.

- What is real in the world of business are only those things that can be measured.

- You can't both make a profit and ground your business decisions in care for human well-being and the health of the planet.

- Business must maximize economic utility at the expense of humanity's potential for living with higher purpose and meaning.

- You must park your soul at the door of your business, as if work can be separated from your larger life's journey.

- *I* and *we* are separate concerns.

Remember, your worldview is a story you tell yourself, and the choice to change parts of that story is available to you at any time.

ESSENTIAL NONSEPARATION

"Don't ask what the world needs. Ask what makes you come alive, and go do it. Because what the world needs is people who have come alive."

—Howard Thurman

Isaac Newton is rightly esteemed as a beacon of scientific inquiry, but did you know that he publicly supported the calculation that God created the world on October 23, 4004 BCE? This is not to mock or belittle Newton; it is to remind us that the current dominant Western understanding of the world—or what Einstein referred to as the "optical delusion" of our separation—might someday prove to be just as narrow a perspective as this particular calculation of Newton.

The fact that the science of quantum physics has revealed a phenomenon in which entangled particles remain connected in such a way that actions performed on one affect the other even though they are separated by a vast distance tells us that there is something connecting the two particles that science can't yet explain or that there is some type of information moving faster than the speed of light between them. This lack of understanding does not mean this reality doesn't exist, only that it is not yet explainable.

Einstein, near the end of his life, stated that he wished he had spent more time studying the mystics. Perhaps this was because Einstein came to appreciate that mystics had perceived the truth of our essential nonseparation, a perspective different from his own.

Nikola Tesla, another paragon of scientific knowledge, hinted at the same notion when he said, "The day science begins to study nonphysical phenomena, it will make more progress in one decade than in all the previous centuries of its existence." In effect, Tesla was suggesting that progress is more dependent on spiritual and mystical matters than on science.

Dev Tandon, Emily Hunt Turner, and the countless other exemplars of Generation Re are at the vanguard of those who have seen through the optical delusion of our separation, and as is demonstrated through their ambitious actions, they are living a new world into existence.

"Just beyond
yourself.

It's where
you need
to be.

Half a step
into
self-forgetting
and the rest
restored
by what
you'll meet."

—*David Whyte*[13]
The Bell and the Blackbird, © *2019*

Chapter 2

REIMAGINE

*"The man who has no imagination
has no wings."*

—MUHAMMAD ALI

A lmost everything we now assume as a given—from politics and poetry to commerce and the very chair you are sitting on—was first formed in the imagination. If we are to call forth the immense potentialities of the future, it is imperative we engage the generative power of our imagination; it is the seed of transformation that can create something from nothing.

REIMAGINING OUR PLACE IN THE WORLD

*"Imagination must precede implementation,
for what we can imagine we can build."*

—WALTER BRUEGGEMANN

The first atlas, the *Theatrum Orbis Terrarum,* or *Theater of the Orb of the World* (see figure 2.1) became available for purchase 450 years ago in Antwerp. Produced by Abraham Ortelius, the publication of the book was a seminal event, because its 53 exquisitely beautiful maps represented the sum total of the world's then known cartography, and it allowed the reader to imagine the totality of Earth for the first time.

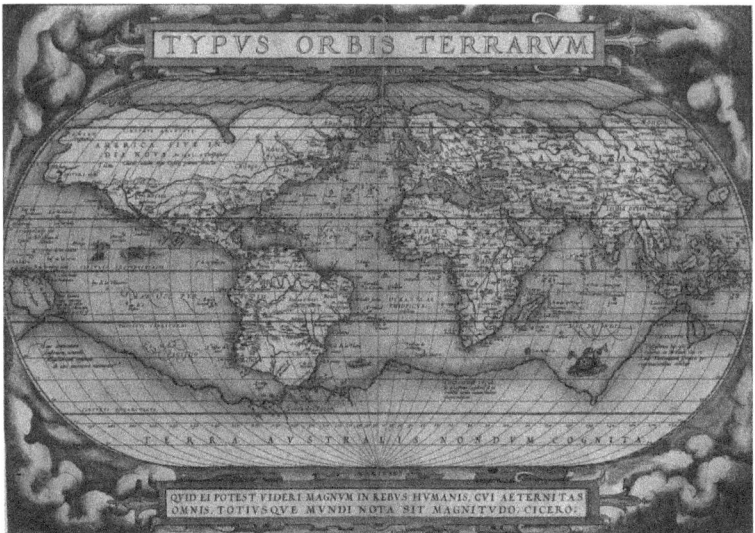

Figure 2.1. Theatrum Orbis Terrarum.

People could now mentally locate themselves in the physical world, allowing them to come to a new understanding of their place in it. While this new knowledge stimulated extraordinary progress (for many but not all people), something less noticeable was happening: The world of measurement began to overtake the world of metaphor.

As was noted in the introduction, the T-O map and other maps existed prior to Ortelius's atlas, but it could be said that these older maps were more comprehensive (more "true"), because they sought to anchor the viewer not just in a physical place but also in history, myth, anthropology, and scripture. The maps told deeper and richer stories, based on shared meaning rather than just an accurate portrayal of the physical world.

If, as Charles Eisenstein expresses, we are to reimagine the more beautiful world we know is possible, we must first reimagine new ways of *seeing* the world in order that we may reimagine new ways of *being* in the world. One place to begin is by reimagining the stories we tell ourselves about what is possible.

ALEX HONNOLD AND REIMAGINING THE IMPOSSIBLE

"What we need is more people who specialize in the impossible."

—THEODORE ROETHKE

Most people look at the daunting 3,000-foot vertical face of El Capitan in Yosemite National Park and can't imagine climbing it. In fact, it was not scaled until 1958. Fewer still can imagine climbing it barehanded, without the aid of ropes, harnesses, or protective equipment, a feat known as *free soloing*. This does not mean it is impossible.

On June 6, 2017, with a film crew nervously capturing every moment of his historic ascent, Alex Honnold scaled the sheer face of El Capitan in less than four hours in an act that defied common perception and conventional wisdom.[1] It typically takes experienced climbers with equipment five to seven days to scale El Capitan.

How did Honnold accomplish his monumental feat? It was an elaborate, complicated, and risky undertaking, but Honnold first imagined that he *could* do it. His thoughts became words, and his words developed into a plan. The plan then manifested itself into a series of discrete actions.

Honnold learned every crack and crevice along his route, and over a period of years, he relentlessly rehearsed each move until he had committed every minuscule move down to muscle memory. In the evenings, he further cemented his plan by visualizing the entire sequence until he had memorized every move he had to make during the daring ascent.

In this sense, Honnold's plan became a habit, and his physical and mental preparation created his destiny, which was to become the first human to free solo El Capitan. The feat has been called the moon landing of rock climbing, and others have labeled it the single greatest athletic achievement in human history.

DRAMATIC REIMAGININGS

"It is better to believe than to disbelieve, for, in doing so, your imagination can begin to bring everything into the realm of possibility."

—ALBERT EINSTEIN

We can't all be Alex Honnold, nor would most of us want to be, but his extraordinary accomplishment reminds us of the importance of imagination. It stretches the boundaries of what is possible and even of what is thought possible.

The past, though, is just a prelude. Never before in human history has society had a better set of tools with which to reimagine the world. From advances in renewable energy, high-speed internet, mobile communication devices, and 3D printing to developments in artificial intelligence, blockchain technology, biotechnology, and nanotechnology, the raw material for reimagining the future has never been greater.

But these physical and scientific tools pale in comparison to what resides in the human mind, heart, and spirit. Is it unreasonable to reimagine a world that works for everyone? What about a world where racism, sexism, child abuse, and poverty are all reimagined out of existence?

What is in your heart—a world without malnutrition, chronic disease, homelessness or prison systems? What about a world without walls or borders or where trash is obsolete and food is healthier, tastier, and more affordable? Could a world exist where the lakes, rivers, and oceans are no longer polluted and where sentient creatures are recognized as having rights on par with humans? What about a world where half the planet is set aside in the name of biodiversity so that all creatures may be assured of not prematurely facing extinction?

It is all possible. There are individuals, organizations, entrepreneurs, and corporations engaged in exactly this type of reimagining at this very moment. Let's highlight one individual and a few companies and communities that are reimagining money, capitalism, and energy.

Reimagining money

> *"It is difficult to get a man to understand something
> when his salary depends upon his not understanding it."*
>
> —UPTON SINCLAIR

Today, we take money for granted, as though it has always existed and as though the world could not function without it. From an evolutionary perspective, however, money is a relatively new phenomena, having only made an appearance 5,000 years ago in the form of the Mesopotamian shekel. But someone first had to imagine money as a new and improved method of exchanging value. This advance then led others to imagine into existence commerce, trade, banks, and—ultimately—everything from complex junk bond derivatives to Venmo.

At its most basic level, money is a social construct—a concept that has no existence outside of its construction through human interaction; it exists only because humans agree that it exists. Money only has value because an authority—typically, a national government—has decreed it so. Even gold, a more tangible and objective medium, only has value because it is deemed, by virtue of its beauty and scarcity, to be valuable.

Most money today is fiat money, currency that is maintained and managed by national governments for the purpose of facilitating commerce. One of the primary ways for a society to create money is for banks to lend it into existence. Things begin to unravel here, and a disconnection is seeded.

There is little argument over money's practical utility in allowing individuals and businesses to effectively and efficiently exchange their labors and skills in return for goods and services they need or want. Money, though, is neither a neutral nor a passive medium of exchange. It can have unintended consequences. The first problem is this: In order to make a profit for its service of lending money, banks charge interest. The requirement to pay back the loan creates artificial pressure on economic growth, because it requires borrowers to service the debt. The second issue is that governments, in their quest for efficiency, create an underappreciated and often unacknowledged disconnection between value and money. It is an almost unquestioned assumption that fiat money (the US dollar, the Euro, the Yen, etc.) is the only way to efficiently facilitate commerce. Accepting this assumption at face value forces society to place an arbitrary value on many things, while utterly ignoring the value of other important things.

Consider this example: Under the existing system, the labor of a home health aide is $15 an hour, which, in dollars, is equal to the cost of repairing a broken window (minimally) or the price of five gallons of gas (at $3 a gallon). But is the loving care the home health aide provides a patient or the comfort they provide to family members adequately captured in their hourly wage?

At an even deeper level, our existing system of monetization undermines the reality of the interconnectedness of things by failing to connect the dots of the truer costs. What are the hidden costs (emotional and otherwise) behind the broken window if it was caused by a hailstorm or by vandalism? And is the external cost of the carbon dioxide that the fuel disperses into the atmosphere reflected in its price? If our currency doesn't capture the intangible value of the aide caring for an elderly resident or the costs behind the invisible roots of vandalism, and if the long-term costs of CO_2 emissions on the health of the planet and future generations are not reflected in the price of gasoline, it is not difficult to see why a number of people choose not to pay attention to those matters: It just doesn't pay. Turning a blind eye to these realities is not an act without harm. Each shortcoming erodes society by weakening connections between people, communities, and the planet.

It does not need to be this way, and a number of people, organizations, and communities are reimagining money and the role it can play in drawing us closer to the things that truly matter but that are difficult, if not impossible, to properly evaluate with money.

One such person was Bernard Lietaer. Lietaer was a brilliant man whose research was instrumental in getting the United States off the gold standard in the early 1970s and who later helped develop the European Currency Unit (the precursor to the Euro). But Lietaer's real breakthrough idea was his ability to reimagine what money was and what it could do.

His key insight was that money is nothing more than an understanding within a community to use a standardized item as a medium of exchange, and, as such, there was no reason for society to limit itself to just one medium of exchange. Through the development of innovative local currencies, communities could improve solidarity among neighbors, foster intergenerational care, inspire lifestyles that reduce carbon emissions, and even support a culture of cooperation instead of competition.

The neighborhood of Rabat, a lower-income section of Ghent, Belgium, has put Lietaer's ideas into action in an effort to better address local communities' needs, foster interconnection, and make the community stronger and more resilient. Through a comprehensive survey, city officials discovered that what a sizable number of residents in the neighborhood really desired was the ability to grow their own food. Because most of the residents live in tall apartment towers, this wasn't possible. The city did, however, have a number of plots of unused land. Lietaer saw an opportunity to connect the residents' unmet demand for growing their own food with the undervalued land the neighborhood possessed.

With Lietaer's assistance, Rabat created a currency called Torekes (which means "little towers" in Flemish). His system allows the residents of the neighborhood to earn the currency for a wide variety of community-strengthening actions, including using renewable energy, participating in car pools, planting public gardens, collecting litter, and fixing public buildings. The Torekes earned could then be used to rent a plot of land for gardening.[2]

In addition to helping the residents save money and eat healthier, it beautified the community by filling once-vacant lots with fresh vegetables. But Lietaer understood Torekes could do even more. Citizens can now use Torekes to pay rent, as well as buy products and services from local shops and stores. The former helps local residents save money and create wealth, while the latter strengthens the community by keeping money circulating within the neighborhood.

Near the end of his life, Lietaer said, "I sometimes feel like a flying fish who has had the opportunity to take a bird's eye view of the water in which we swim, and is now trying to report back to its fellow fish and explain what it has learned about what we usually cannot see."[3] What Lietaer was saying in this context is that community currencies are a big trend, and both communities and businesses need to understand how they can be leveraged to help actualize more of what enables humans to flourish.

The main barrier to these new currencies, he added, was that most people can't imagine an alternative financial system is possible. Fortunately, a legion of Generation Re members are among those who are capable of reimagining a more fair, free, and fluid financial system. Local currencies are a rapidly growing trend, with systems already operational throughout the world.

A PHRASE TO RETIRE: "I CAN'T IMAGINE"

How often have you uttered or heard another person say the phrase "I can't imagine"? Often, the phrase is used as a way for a person to express their opinion that an idea is unlikely, undesirable, or improbable. The problem with the expression is that it can dampen a person's or an organization's willingness to explore alternatives and imagine new possibilities.

The next time you feel like saying you "can't imagine" something, challenge yourself to think again. It is quite possible that someone on this vast planet of almost 8 billion people is already imagining a better, healthier, or more holistic way of doing things.

WePower, an innovative European start-up, is reimagining a world without banks or debt. The company is using blockchain technology (a decentralized digital ledger) to radically rethink how renewable energy plants can be financed without the use of a bank and without requiring debt.

In simple terms, investors—using fiat money—purchase a blockchain token that represents one kilowatt-hour of power. This conventional investment provides renewable energy companies with the necessary capital to finance the construction of their wind, solar, or microgrid platforms without using the services of a traditional bank and without going into debt. The investors, in turn, receive access to renewable energy in the amount of their tokens.

Brooklyn Microgrid, a subsidiary of LO3 Energy, is taking blockchain technology a step further by reimagining a future world where traditional energy producers are replaced by peer-to-peer cooperatives and prosumers (people who produce their own renewable energy), who then sell their energy at a discount or share it freely.

At a basic level, Brooklyn Microgrid uses the recording power of blockchain, the digital ledger, to track the output of people's solar panels and then allows the producers of this energy to swap and share energy with people and organizations in their neighborhood.

Brooklyn Microgrid's peer-to-peer network points toward a sustainable and equitable future whereby even those who can't afford to produce renewable energy in their own home may be the recipients of the excess power prosumers do not need.

In the not-too-distant future, it is possible that millions of homeowners and businesses will be producing so much renewable energy that they can easily and rapidly transfer the electrons they have harvested from the sun or the wind to people in their community. In doing so, these prosumers may replace today's existing energy producers.

Reimagining capitalism

"Human creativity is unlimited. It is the capacity of humans to make things happen which didn't happen before. Creativity provides the key to solving our social and economic problems."

—MUHAMMAD YUNUS, founder of Grameen Bank and pioneer of microcredit and microfinance

Just as money is a social construct, so too is capitalism. It is commonly defined as being based on private ownership for profit. Embedded in this definition are a set of deeply held assumptions around competitive markets, legal systems, and the recognition of property rights, the voluntary exchange of labor and wages, and profits. Not one of these assumptions is fixed, and a handful of corporations, individuals, and organizations are working to reimagine capitalism.

In December 2018, outdoor clothing retailer Patagonia announced it was changing its mission statement to "we're in business to save our home planet."[4] The statement was more than just corporate grandstanding; it was a cannon shot across the bow of capitalism. It signaled that the company, and its 80-year-old founder, Yvon Chouinard, was serious about reimagining business and creatively altering the assumed rules of capitalism.

Patagonia has always been a different kind of company. Chouinard long ago had two key insights that allowed him to reimagine what a business could and should be. First, he understood that business does not need to be ruled by only one metric—profits. Second, if a business wants to flourish over the long term, it also needs to serve humankind.

Since its founding, Patagonia has stayed true to these insights. In the late 1970s, when the company realized its most profitable product (climbing pitons) was doing irreparable damage to the mountains, it stopped selling the product immediately and worked to redesign a new type of piton that did minimal damage.[5] The revised and improved product ushered in the era of clean climbing.

In the early 1980s, Patagonia helped develop Synchilla, a polyester fleece made from recycled plastic bottles, to manufacture vests in an effort to mitigate the growing problem of plastic waste. Later in that decade, it began donating 10 percent of its pre-tax profits to grassroots environmental organizations.[6] In the 1990s and 2000s, Patagonia increased the number of repair shops it operated to help customers repair old clothing. In the 2010s, it unveiled its innovative "Don't buy this jacket" advertising campaign as a way to discourage overconsumption and then followed this up by creating Worn Wear, an e-commerce market for used goods.

If Patagonia's only metric was profit, it would have consistently encouraged its customers to buy new products. Instead, the company actively works to reduce its environmental footprint by helping customers become more conscious about the impact of their purchasing decisions. In the process, it also helps its customers save money by prolonging the use of their existing Patagonia products.

Under the leadership of Rose Marcario (who retired at the end of 2020 and who clearly led by the ethos of Generation Re), Patagonia continued to live into and expand on its founding principles. For example, the company has funded a venture capital arm, Tin Shed Ventures, to support small, environmentally responsible ventures such as Wild Idea Buffalo, which raises bison in a humane way while also restoring grasslands. It has also created Recraft, a new brand focused exclusively on repurposing old clothing into premium products.

Marcario was also instrumental in advancing the company in foresightful and less conventional directions. For example, Marcario understood that, if Patagonia was serious about saving the planet, it needed like-minded people to achieve this goal. Therefore, the company adopted a radical new hiring policy and made the decision to hire the person "who's most committed to saving the planet *no matter what*."[7]

The change is paradigm shifting. No longer is the company hiring the most technically proficient person. Instead, it is hiring the person most committed to the mission. Patagonia is taking a calculated risk that, by hiring only people who have been living their inner convictions, it can achieve maximum external impact toward its new mission.

The new mission statement has resulted in one additional monumental change. In 2018, Marcario went to her product team and asked, "What do you think will be the biggest risk to our business in the next 30 years?"[8] The team replied, "Soil health." This is because of the role soil plays in everything from the creation of cotton for its products to its ability to help combat climate change by serving as a carbon sink.

The question and the resulting answer set in motion a series of changes that will materially affect the future direction of Patagonia. The company reviewed its supply chains to make sure all suppliers understood and were working on improving soil health. As a result, it developed new technologies (such as recycled down) that would alleviate pressure on soil health, and it expanded free trade certification standards to ensure it was working only with partners who were equally committed to saving soil.

The most important and most profound change is that Patagonia is now actively positioning itself for an extraordinary transition. In the near future, the company believes its sustainable food offshoot, Patagonia Provisions, will be bigger than its apparel business.

Patagonia understood that if it was serious about its mission to save the planet, its customers must learn how to recycle, repurpose, and repair their clothing and, if it is successful in achieving this goal, the growth of its apparel business line must decline over time. The company also determined that agriculture was the area in which it could have the biggest impact on achieving its mission.

As a result, regenerative agriculture, which has long been important within Patagonia, is now a top priority. If done right, the company will capture more carbon than it emits, which will help mitigate climate change. Regenerative agriculture will also place the company at the vanguard of a revolution where growing numbers of farmers are eliminating chemicals through the strategic use and rotation of cover crops. As an added benefit, the cover crops will assist small farmers in supplementing their annual income with an additional source of income in the off-season.

In many ways, Yvon Chouinard could be considered an elder statesman for Generation Re. He has been quoted as saying, "Every single company in the world has to do the same thing."[9] By reimagining what a business can be, Chouinard and Marcario are not only inviting other imaginal cells to follow Patagonia's lead, but they are also demonstrating how a business can foster an imaginative culture and create a successful, regenerative company.

Reimagining affordable housing

Chouinard is not alone in his quest to reimagine business. Gospatric Home, another octogenarian, embodied the ethos of Generation Re long before the existence of any efforts to identify and galvanize others to embrace this spirit of regeneration. Home died in 2020 to little fanfare. This was unfortunate, because he may well be one of the most influential people you have never heard of. Quite literally, hundreds of thousands of individuals in London, one of the world's most expensive cities, today live in affordable housing due to his efforts.

In 1963, with only $80 in hand, Gospatric Home cofounded L&Q, a not-for-profit housing association that, today, has a $43 billion property portfolio and houses five percent of London's population.[10] In the beginning, though, Home wanted to do nothing more than help homeless families find safe, clean, and modest housing.

He began by seeking to understand the plight of London's homeless population by visiting them in person. At one location, Home saw a young child with a large rat bite on her swollen cheek. With that as his sole inspiration, he had found, in his words, "a problem to solve" and "motivation for life."

With the modest investment, Home placed a down payment on a single property and set about improving the house to see if it could serve as a pilot project. As an outsider, Home (who had only recently returned from the Korean War, where he served as an officer in the British Army) was not limited by conventional wisdom. In fact, his naïveté inspired his first leap of imagination: A property company could thrive by putting social values, social impact, and the long-term interest of the community at the center of a business plan, instead of merely profits.

With the benefit of a beginner's mind, Home was free to reimagine the field of affordable housing in other ways. He looked for unconventional properties and innovative ways to finance the projects. He was also free to experiment and take risks, occasionally pushing regulators beyond their comfort zone.

Over its 57 years of existence, L&Q has established a model that roughly follows this formula: 25 percent of its housing is for private rent, and 25 percent of its properties are built for outright sale. This profit-generating half of the company's portfolio then serves to support and sustain the other half, 25 percent of which is subsidized housing, and the other 25 percent is for submarket ownership.

In an interview near the end of his life, Home explained that what he really hoped to create was a sense of togetherness and unity. It was important for him that people of different economic classes lived in close proximity to one another because it created a sense of community.

Equally important, Gospatric Home built a regenerative model that is capable of growing well into the future. The company has plans to double its portfolio by bringing an additional 100,000 units of affordable housing into existence within the next decade.

Home's personal net worth isn't known, but it is clear from his life's work that that number never mattered to him. What mattered most was the value he contributed to society. In this sense, Home was (and remains even after his death) a cultural billionaire in terms of the social impact he created by reimagining the field of affordable housing and creating homes for hundreds of thousands of people.

Reimagining energy

In 2014, Connie Stacey was taking her two young twins for a stroll in hopes of getting them to nap when she walked by a construction site in her neighborhood that was using a loud, smelly diesel generator to produce electricity. The chance encounter caused Stacey, an IT professional, to begin imagining a quieter, cleaner alternative.

As she researched the issue, Stacey learned that over 1.2 billion people on the planet live at energy tier zero, which is essentially living by candlelight, and another 2.6 billion still burn biomass for cooking.[11] To put a finer point on it, almost half the planet lives in energy poverty.

This reality caused Stacey to ask why dependable, affordable power isn't available to everyone. Unsatisfied with what she found, Stacey left her full-time job to start a company that produced a silent, fumeless portable battery that is scalable, sustainable, and affordable.

The result is the Grengine UltraLite, a stackable battery that can be clipped together like LEGO bricks to meet almost any power need, from powering a ventilator to an entire city. The Grengine can be powered from an outlet, a solar panel, or even a stationary bike if necessary. Moreover, the Grengine was designed to be so easy to use that a person need not be an electrician or an engineer to operate the equipment. From allowing schools to be lit into the evening and powering the internet and smartphones to freeing up people from having to gather fuel for cooking, the Grengine holds the possibility of eliminating energy poverty across the world.

SKILLS AND INSIGHTS FOR REIMAGINING

*"In the beginner's mind there are many possibilities,
in the expert's there are few."*

—SHUNRYU SUZUKI

Reimagining the future of anything—capitalism, business, energy production, or the way you express yourself in the world—can be facilitated through a beginner's mind. A beginner's mind involves seeing life with a sense of wonder or, alternatively, having an attitude of openness or eagerness and a lack of preconceptions when studying a subject. This way of perceiving underlies the success of Generation Re. The smarter a person thinks they are, the less open-minded they tend to be, which inhibits potential for the inspiration that can lead to creative breakthroughs.

In a study conducted by Professor Victor Ottati, at Loyola University Chicago, people who perceived themselves to be experts exhibit more close-minded behavior.[12] He hypothesizes that experts feel they have earned the privilege of holding more dogmatic beliefs and opinions.

In the slower-moving world of yesteryear, this wasn't necessarily a fatal character flaw. In today's rapidly changing world, it is potentially lethal, because it can hold people and organizations back from the important and necessary work of reimagining new possibilities.

As an analogy, there is a famous study that has been repeated on thousands of individuals, young and old. In the test, participants were asked, "How many uses are there for a shoe?" and "How many uses can you think of for a paper clip?" Most people came up with between 1 and 15 ideas, but a rare few were capable of discerning upward of 200 potential applications.[13] The latter were categorized as geniuses in divergent thinking.

More important, of nearly 1,500 kindergartners who were tested, a staggering 98 percent were rated geniuses in divergent thinking. When those same children were retested five years later, only 32 percent sustained the genius rating. By the time they were 15 years old, a mere 10 percent retained this level of creativity. The rate among adults was even worse: Only two percent retained the label of genius.

It seems that the accumulation of more knowledge led to less imagination. This may have been what Albert Einstein was trying to address when he said, "Imagination is more important than knowledge. Knowledge is limited. Imagination encircles the world."

If we are to reimagine a new and better future, it is imperative that more of us cultivate a beginner's mind. Here are eight practices that can help cultivate this state of open inquisitiveness:

Question everything

The beginner's mind is our original state of mind and one we will be called to return to with increasing frequency because the future won't come with many answers. Instead, questions will be the best and surest way to explore and probe the future. In his 2014 book *A More Beautiful Question*, Warren Berger points out that the peak age for asking questions is four years old. At this stage, children are curious about almost everyone and everything. Businesses and business leaders should strive to be the same. Try incorporating these childlike questions back into your repertoire: *Tell me more about _____? Why? Why not?* And, *Says who?* Recall the examples of the blockchain start-ups reimagining the financing and distribution of energy without money. Traditional bankers and energy executives may balk at the possibility of this future happening, but *Why not?* and *Says who?*

Epilogg is a new start-up that is reimagining the obituary. Instead of charging grieving families an exorbitant fee to place a few hundred words about the life of the deceased in the paper for a day or two, Epilogg has created a digital platform that allows friends and family members to post old photos, letters, and videos that more intimately capture the depth, vitality, and fullness of a person's life for a fraction of the cost—or no cost at all. Moreover, because it is a digital document anyone can add to at any time, it becomes more of a living document.

Challenge assumptions

The British polymath and philosopher Bertrand Russell once said, "In all affairs, it is a healthy thing to hang a question mark on long-held assumptions." This is solid advice. Patagonia, long ago, challenged the assumption of allowing profits to be the sole determinant of success, and its reimaginings resulted in a number of innovative and unconventional methods of operation. The company has also gained a legion of loyal and lifelong fans because of its more holistic approach.

An old but still relevant example is the curious case of the suitcase with wheels. A wheeled suitcase was not invented until 1972, almost three years after Apollo 11 first landed humans on the moon. It is a wonderful reminder that innovations need not be profound or complicated.

Practice challenging your assumptions about capitalism, your industry, your customers, your competitors, your pricing, and your business models. To begin, you might consider asking yourself a rather high-level question: Do your assumptions about these things and your resulting decisions lead to decision-making ends that are fundamentally life giving or life depleting?

Gain perspective

One of the surest ways to provoke the imagination is to seek out environments in which you have no experience. Also remember that what you experience and the story you create about it are just one perspective, one interpretation. In her 2020 book, *Manifesto for a Moral Revolution*, Jacqueline Novogratz recounts the story of d.light, a solar lantern company her social impact investing firm was backing in an effort to bring affordable and clean (nonpolluting) light to Africa. When Novogratz traveled to Pakistan, she sat down with the women in the communities to describe the many benefits of the technology. She was told that, due to the stifling heat in Pakistan, what they really needed were fans, not lights. Instead of trying to convince the women of the value of light (the women said they already worked long enough hours), d.light listened to their concerns. The company reimagined how an affordable, clean-powered fan could be manufactured, marketed, and distributed—and they did it.

Be naive

The word *naive* commonly suggests ignorance or simplemindedness, but it is better thought of as a type of open-mindedness. Gospatric Home, the founder of L&Q, credited his success in providing homes for hundreds of thousands of low-income individuals in London to his naïveté. He "didn't know what he didn't know," so he was free to challenge the status quo and ask simple questions. Patagonia did much the same when it adopted its new hiring policy that selected people based not on their skill but, rather, on their passion for saving the planet. It may sound naive, but the company was open to the idea that skills can be taught, but passion can't.

Drop labels and identification

Humans are social animals, and it is natural to want to identify with others. Developing a beginner's mind requires people to drop their methods of identification for a period of time. Whether you consider yourself a liberal or conservative, athlete or artist, vegan or omnivore, or any of the other scores of labels people use to identify themselves and others, they all serve to place our thinking into a constricted box. If dropping a long-held label is too difficult, try putting on a new and different label, and then reimagine the world from that perspective. Gospatric Home created a $43 billion property company because he saw the world from the perspective of a four-year-old child.

Another example can be found in the wisdom of Reed Hastings, who, when he founded Netflix, consciously decided not to use the word *mail* in the company name because he did not want to limit himself or his team to think the company's only mission was to deliver movie DVDs to consumers by mail.[14] This flexibility allowed Netflix to more easily transition into streaming and then into the content creation business.

Redefine failures as learning opportunities

The skill of walking can only be learned through trial and error. The emerging future of our imagination is no different. No one labels an infant a failure for stumbling. The same approach is necessary as business reimagines its way into the future. Not everything will work, and companies, entrepreneurs, and innovators must experiment by falling down and getting back up.

One innovative approach to help overcome people's fear of failure and risk was created by Tor Myhren, who, as a senior vice president at Grey New York, instituted the heroic failure award to reward risk-taking. By reframing setbacks and failures into learning opportunities, she effectively cultivated a culture that fostered a beginner's mind and drove innovation. Bernard Lietaer was also adamant that experimentation and failure would be necessary for the development of new, innovative community currencies for the simple reason that society still has so much to learn before it can walk—and then run—into this new future.

Become an amateur juggler

The word *amateur* is derived from the Latin word for "lover" (*amator*). It references doing something for the love of it rather than for money. In his book *Range: Why Generalists Triumph in a Specialized World*, David Epstein notes that Nobel laureates, when compared with other scientists, are "at least 22 times more likely to partake as an amateur actor, dancer, magician, or other type of performer."[15] The expansion of skills, including those a person is not accomplished at, opens up new neural pathways and allows that person to make new and unexpected connections. The act of juggling has been found in a number of neuroscience studies to both alter and strengthen a person's ability to form new neural pathways, improving their ability to think and imagine creatively.[16]

Sit under the stars

Years ago, while speaking at an event in Savannah, Jack had an opportunity to sit on a panel with a professor at the Savannah School of Design. The topic was "imagining the future," and the professor told a poignant story of how his job of teaching the subject of product design had grown increasingly difficult over the years. He explained that, since he began his career 25 years earlier, he had been asking incoming freshmen one simple question. Every year, fewer students responded affirmatively. The question was this: How many of you have spent a night camping under the stars?

From the professor's perspective, the students' responses were a proxy for a powerful idea: How many students had been exposed to the transformative power of awe? If they hadn't been so exposed, the professor felt his ability to effectively teach design was compromised, because his students' minds, in a sense, had become confined.

The professor believed that sitting under the night sky also acts to engage the imagination. First, it quiets the ego. When exposed to the vastness of the universe, he felt, the sense of being an individual recedes, and one's focus tends to shift from the self toward wider and deeper connections.

Second, he felt that awe prompts intellectual openness and expands creativity. It is difficult to sit under the vast mystery of the universe and not feel humbled by all that we don't know. This was important from the professor's perspective, because when people are content, they tend to rely more on existing knowledge to generate ideas. When in awe, they are better able to step through existing filters and move beyond existing assumptions to generate new thoughts, see previously invisible pathways, and imagine new possibilities.

If the future is to be awesome—in the sense of inspiring awe—it is essential to have the capacity to both see and take in awe-worthy things. Fortunately, the night sky offers a portal available to everyone.

If you live in a city where light pollution makes seeing the night sky difficult, don't worry. Sitting under the stars isn't the only way to strengthen your imagination muscles. Henry Miller was on to something when he wrote, "The moment one gives close attention to anything, even a blade of grass, it becomes a mysterious, awesome, indescribably magnificent world in itself." If you are able to stay present to the everyday awe that surrounds us, you will have taken the first and, perhaps, most important step toward reimagining a better future.

A MATTER OF PERSPECTIVE

How would you answer the following questions?

- How much larger is Africa than Greenland?

- Which is larger, Europe or South America?

- How much larger is Alaska than Mexico?

Now, if necessary, consult the Mercator projection map in figure 2.2.

How did your answers stack up to the sizes represented by this map? Were you close? If so, congratulations. But the Mercator projection, which has been in standard use in schools, universities, and the media for centuries, is a lie. It badly distorts reality, because it is nowhere near scale.

The answers to the questions above will provide some insight into the matter: Africa is 14 times larger than Greenland, South America is approximately twice the size of Europe, and Mexico is actually more than one million square miles larger than Alaska.

But you may be forgiven if you couldn't surmise the correct answers from the Mercator map.

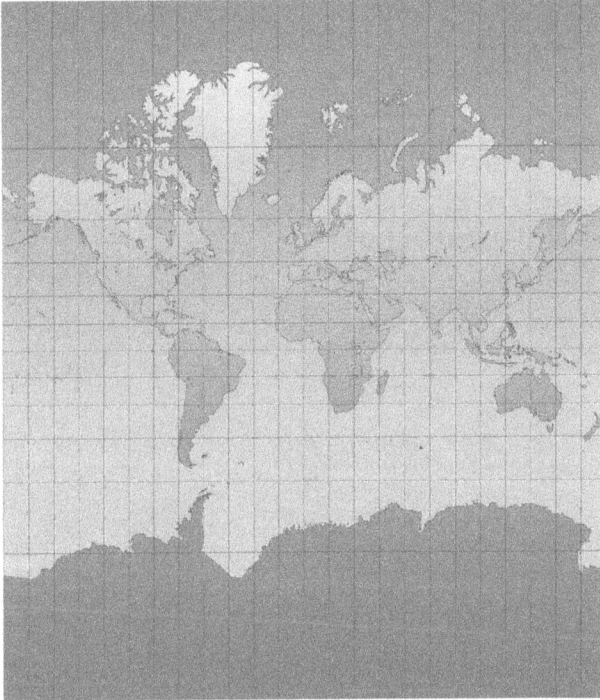

Figure 2.2. A Mercator projection map.

The correct answers can be better discerned using the Gall–Peters projection map (see figure 2.3). This projection was developed by Arno Peters, a German filmmaker, and James Gall, a nineteenth-century Scotsman who Peters borrowed much of his early cartography work from.

In spite of its odd appearance, the Gall–Peters map has the advantage of being an equal-area map. It accurately portrays sizes, although it does distort the shape of countries and continents, because it stretches vertically near the equator and horizontally near the poles. This gives Africa a more elongated shape, and Antarctica appears to flatten out across the entire bottom of the map.

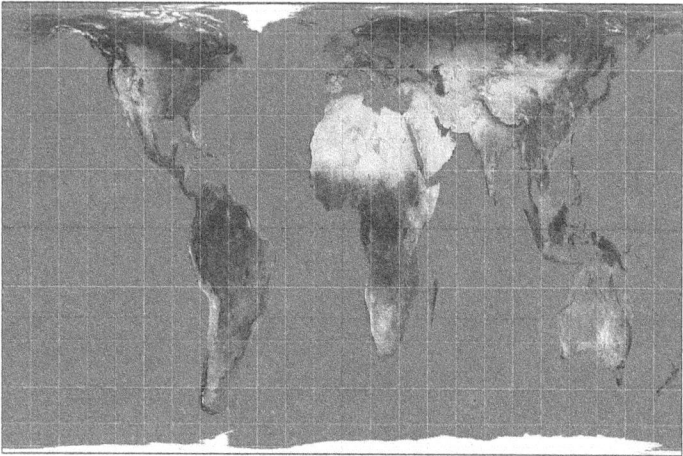

Figure 2.3. A Gall–Peters projection map.

There are over 50 different projection maps, and the most recent addition is the doubled-sided disk map in figure 2.4. It was created in 2020 by J. Richard Gott, an astrophysicist at Princeton University; Robert Vanderbei, a mathematician and professor at Princeton; and David Goldberg, a professor of physics at Drexel University. The two-sided map looks like an old vinyl record, but it has the distinction of doing the best job of minimizing all of the various distortions any two-dimensional map will possess. These distortions can include local shapes, area sizes, distances, and boundary cuts.

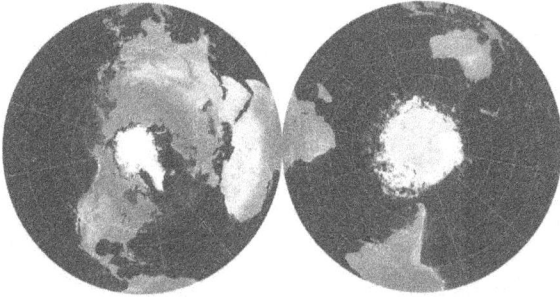

Figure 2.4. A two-sided disk map.

Now consider the "upside-down" map in figure 2.5. It is rare that people from the Northern Hemisphere ever view a world map from this perspective, but it is critical to understand that this is an equally legitimate way to view the world. The only reason so many of us don't view the world from this perspective is because Gerardus Mercator was from Europe, so he placed Europe on the top half of the map. It was simply a matter of perspective.

Figure 2.5. Change your perspective of the world.

The truth is this: From outer space, there is no north, south, east, or west. Even these directions are human constructs designed to help orient us and give us a sense of place—and thus are a matter of perspective. The reality is this: Our image of the world is just one perspective—there are an infinite number of ways to imagine and reimagine it.

Finally, consider the famous *Blue Marble* photo in figure 2.6. It is credited to the three-man crew of Apollo 17 and was snapped on December 7, 1972, during the last piloted mission to the moon. When it was first published, the image of Earth dangling in space captured the global imagination. It is credited to some degree with shifting humanity's consciousness toward sustainable, holistic, and conscious living, because many people, for the first time ever, saw a world that transcends national, political, and religious boundaries. In fact, only 15 months after its publication and wide-spread dissemination, it helped spawn the first Earth Day.

Figure 2.6. The Blue Marble.

If Ortelius's *Theater of the Orb of the World* played a role in causing people to see themselves as separate actors on the world's stage, the *Blue Marble* photo may have inspired the opposite reaction. In fact, Edgar Mitchell, who is one of only six men to walk on the moon and one of the few people to have experienced this view firsthand, had such a profound sense of universal connectedness after observing Earth from this perspective that he retired as an astronaut to found the Institute for Noetic Sciences. The term *noetic* comes from the Greek *nous*, meaning "inner wisdom, direct knowing, intuition, or implicit understanding."[17]

This inner wisdom and direct knowledge may have felt more readily accessible to our ancestors, because there were fewer distractions from external knowledge-sources (like the 24/7 news cycle). But intuition feeds our imagination, and we would be wise to reconnect with this source as we go about reimaging the future.

Can you imagine a world where increasing numbers of ordinary people comprehend their highest potential and cooperate to achieve extraordinarily positive things? What is it that you'd like to reimagine?

Chapter 3

REEXAMINE

"We don't see the world as it is,
we see it as we are."

—ANAÏS NIN

I n the mid-nineteenth century, a strange and poorly understood infection was running rampant throughout Europe. In many hospitals, the disease, known as childbed or puerperal fever, was killing 10 percent of all women after childbirth. In spite of many of the best doctors studying it, the disease was believed to be unpreventable.

A break came when a colleague of Ignaz Semmelweis died after cutting his finger with a scalpel he had used while performing an autopsy on a woman who had also succumbed to the disease. Up until that time, the prevailing belief was that the infection affected only women in childbirth.

This anomaly prompted Semmelweis to rigorously examine the issue. As with many paradigm shifts, this one can also trace its roots to the discovery of a new fact that did not fit the prevailing theories. It was Semmelweis's good fortune that his hospital had two separate maternity wards; this proved to be the perfect lab. The only difference between the two wards was that one was staffed by male doctors and medical students, who, in addition to delivering babies, also performed autopsies. The other ward was staffed solely by midwives, who only delivered babies.

The difference in the death rates was staggering. In the ward staffed by the male doctors, the death rate was 10 percent, but it was only 3 percent in the ward staffed by the midwives.[1] This threefold difference led Semmelweis to hypothesize that poisons and tiny, invisible particles from cadavers were causing the disease. He instructed his students and other male doctors to begin sanitizing their hands with chlorinated lime. The death rate immediately fell precipitously.

Armed with these promising results, you might conclude that hospitals across Europe raced to adopt Semmelweis's recommendations. That is not what happened. Many male doctors were offended by the idea that they were the ones giving mothers the infections. It was inconsistent with their idea that a gentleman's hands couldn't be unclean. A few of the clearly ego-driven doctors went so far as to suggest that a more plausible explanation for the higher death rates in their ward was that women were being embarrassed to death by being examined by male doctors.[2]

Most doctors, however, rejected the idea because Semmelweis could not offer sufficient scientific evidence for his theory. Apparently, the compelling data on declining death rates was not enough evidence for them. Instead, they clung to the misguided belief that bad odors in the air—what they called *miasma*—remained the most probable cause of the disease.

In the end, it would be almost 20 years before Louis Pasteur and others would provide the scientific evidence necessary to support Semmelweis's work by explaining the role played by germs. Unfortunately, Semmelweis died before seeing his findings put into widespread practice.

Over time, this story helped coin the term *the Semmelweis effect*, the tendency to reject new information. This is a lesson in itself, but the story is also offered as a cautionary metaphor for the idea that sometimes the invisible is more real than what we think we see.

MEASURING THE RIGHT THINGS

During World War II, Abraham Wald worked for the Statistical Research Group (SRG) at Columbia University. The 23-year-old Hungarian-born statistician and mathematician assessed the vulnerability of Allied aircraft to enemy gunfire. At the time, Germany was dominating the skies over Great Britain, and Allied power officials were intent on finding the best way to protect the Allied aircraft while also keeping them as lightweight and maneuverable as was practical.

As the airplanes returned from their sorties, the SRG's team of quantitatively trained researchers diligently inspected each plane for damage. It was soon apparent from the data that the wings, tails, and fuselages were being struck by bullets at a disproportionately higher rate than the other areas of the plane (see figure 3.1). This led 18 of the 19 members of the team to recommend that the areas most riddled with bullets be reinforced with extra armor.

Figure 3.1. The damage pattern on Allied planes.

Alone, Abraham Wald reached the opposite conclusion. Wald astutely observed that data was only being collected from the planes that had *successfully* completed their missions. It didn't include those planes lost to enemy gunfire. Recognizing that this created a selection bias, he reasoned that the parts of the returning planes *not* riddled with bullet holes were the areas in need of additional fortification.

Wald understood that, if a plane could survive being hit and still make it safely back, then those areas struck were not critical to the plane's survival. To put a different spin on it, the planes were coming back with fewer hits to the engine because those aircraft that had been hit in the engine were *not* coming back. Wald's unique contribution was his ability to see what wasn't there. Unlike the others, he saw the aircraft that *didn't return*.

It was later determined that his insight was instrumental in saving hundreds of Allied flight crews.[3] This might not sound like much, but it is the kind of important detail on which hundreds of lives hinge.

Another important component of the story is this: Getting

the measure right matters. If an army or a business or a country measures the wrong variables, the odds are that it will take the wrong action. At best, this leads to suboptimal results. At worst, the impact can be fatal.

REEXAMINING PROGRESS AND PURPOSE

"The values of the empire are not necessarily the values of humanity."

—MATTHEW FOX

In much the same way that Abraham Wald saw what others were missing and helped win a war, today, a cadre of countries, business associations, corporations, and individuals are reexamining long-held assumptions and challenging conventional notions of progress, profit, purpose, and personal fulfillment. By developing new metrics that better capture what society really values, these exemplars of the ethos of Generation Re are creating better policies for better lives and are driving the world toward a more peaceful and prosperous future.

One of today's more deeply held assumptions is that gross domestic product (GDP) serves as a fair and useful measurement of human progress. The reality is that economists, politicians, policy makers, businesspeople, and citizens have been content with GDP as a tool because it makes sense at an intuitive level (i.e., more money = more prosperity). It also happens to be an easy and convenient way to measure economic consumption and production. Recall, though, how surface-level thinking misled every member of the SRG save for Abraham Wald.

The problem with the GDP is that, in the myopic world-view of economists, when a window is broken, its owner spends money to fix it. This counts as economic growth, and no regard is given to the negative impact on the citizen whose window was broken. In this same way, the billions of dollars spent on opioids are recorded as economic progress in the ledgers of politicians, while the drug's devastating impact is ignored. GDP also misses many of the environmental costs of economic growth. For example, energy produced from fossil fuel is calculated as beneficial economic production, while the costs of dirty water, polluted air, and the loss of biodiversity (animals, plants, insects, fish, etc.) are dismissed as "externalities."

Furthermore, critical components contributing to the health and well-being of a community's social fabric are severely undervalued, including teaching, childcare, and elderly care, while others, such as the fundamental role of motherhood in relation to economic impact, are just beginning to gain attention.

New insights are sometimes found in places we don't often turn to, like the tiny kingdom of Bhutan. Nestled high in the Himalayas, between India and Tibet, the country's king implemented a radical idea in the early 1970s. Rather than just measure economic production, he committed to measuring happiness at the national level. The king's rationale was summarized recently by the country's prime minister: "When we know that monetary wealth and material wealth will not translate to what you actually want in your life—peace of mind and happiness—then why should we target that as our main objective?"[4]

In Bhutan's case, happiness is not a loose, unquantifiable term that merely measures how much the country's citizens smile and laugh. Instead, a list of nine indicators—life span, income, education, time use, good governance, psychological well-being, culture, community vitality, and ecology—have been identified as essential to the happiness of the country's citizens. The country then directs public policies toward achieving these goals.

To be clear, Bhutan is far from the happiest country on the planet; it ranks only 95th out of 156 countries on the United Nations' annual happiness index.[5] Many of its citizens still live in poverty, youth unemployment is on the rise, and its forests are under intense pressure from developers. Nevertheless, since Bhutan challenged the prevailing assumption that economic consumption is the best measure of progress, the life expectancy of its citizens has increased from 50 to 70, extreme poverty has decreased, and gender equality has improved. The country has also introduced meditation into schools and has banned plastic bags and tobacco, making it the first smoke-free country in the world. More recently, Bhutan has mandated that 60 percent of the country's remaining forests be protected, and it has begun subsidizing LED lights and electric vehicles in an effort to sustain its status as a carbon negative country.

Contrast Bhutan with the United States, which has seen GDP increase from $1.27 trillion in 1972 to almost $21 trillion in 2020, adjusted for inflation. But the United States has experienced virtually no change in happiness over the past five decades.[6] Americans are running ever faster on the economic treadmill of progress with no improvement in their overall happiness.

By reexamining the assumption that increased economic consumption is the only goal worthy of measuring, Bhutan has instead chosen to take a more holistic approach, giving as much weight to human flourishing as it does economic wealth. In so doing, it is nudging other countries to reconsider their definition of prosperity. One prominent example is New Zealand, which, in 2019, adopted a "well-being budget." It now places social well-being indicators, including mental health, child poverty, and homelessness, ahead of GDP when it makes spending decisions. Other countries, including the United Kingdom and Costa Rica, have begun to consider similar proposals.

Almost a half century after the late Robert F. Kennedy said, "The gross domestic product . . . measures everything, in short, except that which makes life worthwhile,"[7] it now appears that a small but growing number of countries are working to address this long-mistaken prioritization.

REEXAMINING THE PURPOSE OF BUSINESS

In August 2019, the Business Roundtable, an influential organization made up of the CEOs of major US companies, released a statement redefining their corporate purpose. The "Statement on the Purpose of a Corporation" was signed by 181 members and declared its members "share a fundamental commitment to all of our *stakeholders*" and promised "to deliver value to all of them, for the future success of our companies, our communities, and [our] country."[8]

To some, the statement may sound like common sense. To skeptics, it may appear little more than corporate window dressing. But it reflects a significant shift in corporate philosophy. Since the mid-1990s, the Business Roundtable had previously proclaimed "the paramount duty of management and of boards of directors is to the corporation's stockholders" and that the interests of other stakeholders were only "relevant as a derivative of the duty to stockholders."[9] If we were looking for a statement that demonstrated all that was wrong with capitalism in the first part of the twenty-first century, we needn't look much further than this statement.

In 2020, Larry Fink, the CEO of BlackRock, one of the world's largest financial investment firms, added heft to the Roundtable's announcement by penning a separate letter to CEOs. In it, he declared, "We are on the edge of a fundamental reshaping of finance" and that all businesses must "reassess core assumptions."[10] Primary among these was the assumption that CEOs' and boards of directors' sole fiduciary responsibility rested in serving the shareholders. More succinctly, Fink wrote, "A company cannot achieve long-term profits without embracing purpose and considering a broad range of stakeholders," including the environment.

It was this latter point for which Fink reserved much of his attention. Specifically, he identified climate change as a long-term issue and said that companies, investors, and governments must prepare for a structural reallocation of capital. Climate change, he added, was going to force businesses and governments to reconsider where and how it can deploy capital, because it would transform the value of physical property. Fink also stressed that young individuals, particularly millennials, would soon be occupying a growing number of positions in executive suites and boardrooms, and they were inclined to take a more activist attitude toward the issue.

To add specificity to his message, Fink proclaimed that, in the absence of full disclosure about the risks climate change poses to a company, BlackRock would assume the company and its management had failed to adequately assess that risk and would actively work to remove those leaders it believed who were not executing on their responsibilities to protect the planet. If necessary,

BlackRock also indicated that it would pull its financial support from the company.

Fink later followed up with an even more candid statement: "Stakeholder capitalism is only going to become more and more important, and the companies that focus on all of their stakeholders—their clients, their employees, the society where they work and operate—are going to be the winners of the future."

The World Economic Forum also jumped on board the stakeholder train in 2020 by releasing the Davos Manifesto. Similar in nature to the Business Roundtable's statement, it declared, "The purpose of a company is to engage all of its stakeholders in shared and sustained value creation."[11]

It is too soon to know whether this shift in focus from shareholders to a wider range of stakeholders, including employees, consumers, communities, and the planet, reflects a true change in the heart of business, but stakeholder capitalism is a growing trend. Prudent business leaders will want to begin reexamining the value they bring to the world from an aperture wider than just economic profit.

In the coming years, as more organizations join the trend, the skeptical reader is encouraged to watch for the following signs as proof that the trend is taking root:

- Companies will begin curtailing stock buybacks and begin investing in better pay and benefits for employees.

- Leading companies will resign from influential trade groups that do not support the espoused principles of stakeholder capitalism.

- Leading business schools will stop teaching that shareholder value is the primary or sole focus of business.

- Limits will be placed on CEO pay, and future compensation plans will be focused less on short-term growth and more on achieving values as outlined in environmental, social, and corporate governance principles and the United Nations' 2030 Sustainable Development Goals.

- Individuals representing different stakeholders—union leaders, community leaders, environmental and climate activists—will be placed on boards of directors.

- Companies will be more diligent about measuring outputs such as CO_2 emissions, water use, and waste, and will take active steps to reduce their footprints in those areas.

These trends are gaining steam. As we'll discuss more later, Unilever decided to become net zero carbon 11 years earlier than required under the Paris Agreement on climate change. It has also pledged to disclose the carbon footprint it produces on every package by 2025.[12] Over 100 additional companies have since made the same pledge, committing to three principal areas of action: regular reporting on greenhouse gas emissions, carbon elimination, and credible carbon offsets. On a related note, C. H. Robinson, a leading logistics company, has developed a new tool, Emissions IQ, to help large and small companies measure the carbon footprint of their shipping activities.[13]

Costco's decision in 2019 (prior to the pandemic) to raise its minimum wage to $15 an hour for all of its frontline employees, well above the existing federal minimum wage, is another modest example of a major corporation moving in the direction of stakeholder capitalism. They've since increased hourly wages further, to $17 an hour,[14] and the pandemic has accelerated the acceptance by other companies of similar initiatives that move in the direction of stakeholder capitalism.

In a creative and foresightful move, British energy producer Good Energy announced it would appoint a teenager to its board of directors to help ensure the voice of younger stakeholders are taken into consideration and that the company is taking dedicated steps to serve the long-term interests of future generations.[15]

In early 2021, Veeva, a multibillion-dollar cloud-computing company serving the life sciences industry, became the first publicly traded public benefit corporation. It was a bold decision, because the company, in essence, said to its shareholders that they would no longer be the sole—or even necessarily the primary—focus of the company.

Another company embracing stakeholder capitalism is Danone, the European multinational food production corporation. With $27 billion in annual revenue, its North America subsidiary is already the largest public benefit corporation (PBC) in the world by revenue, balancing the maximization of value to shareholders with a legally binding commitment to a social or environmental mission.[16] What's more, it is committed to becoming one of the first fully certified B Corp multinationals by 2025. As of 2021, 32 Danone entities, representing approximately 50 percent of its global sales, had earned B Corp certification.[17]

Since its founding in 1972, Danone has espoused the idea that a corporation should "be placed at the service of people," and it has long offered a generous vacation policy and retirement plans. By becoming a PBC, however, Danone has taken an evolutionary step beyond short-term profit maximization to serve other stakeholders. Among the many steps it has taken with its entities that have achieved B Corp status is to increase the number of managers who are now evaluated on social and environmental performance. It has also committed to growing the amount of on-site renewable energy it is producing. Danone has also balanced its water footprint by restoring water to streams, redesigning its bottles to be produced with 80 percent sugarcane rather than fossil fuels, and offering long-term contracts to dairy farmers to alleviate market-based volatility, making it easier for them to invest in sustainable activities.

Danone is also aggressively investing in the emerging field of regenerative agriculture, which seeks to increase biodiversity, enhance ecosystems, and enrich the soil. It will do this by employing a variety of techniques, including mandating all of its suppliers to engage in crop rotation, employ innovative cover crops, and use low- or no-tillage practices that limit soil disturbance and enhance carbon sequestration.

The company is putting millions of dollars to work in pursuit of these goals. It is providing loans and grants to dairy farmers to help them become more energy efficient and to convert to renewable energy sources. It is also investing in experimental feeds that could help reduce methane, a potent greenhouse gas, and is working to restore forest and prairie systems to further offset its carbon usage. By 2025, Horizon Organics, one of Danone's leading subsidiaries, is expected to become carbon positive.

Large corporations, however, are not the only ones reexamining the integration of human values at work.

REEXAMINING THE ROLE OF PEOPLE

Jos De Blok was burned out and discouraged in his job as a nurse. Under the Netherlands' home healthcare system, De Blok had been stripped of his professional independence in diagnosing and assessing clients' needs and was forced to spend much of his time tracking and documenting his activities. Mostly, though, he was frustrated that the human bond between the patient and the nurse was being lost.

De Blok resolved to do something about it, and in 2006, he and four other nurses started Buurtzorg (which, in Dutch, means "neighborhood care") with one purpose in mind: to separate human care from the administrative process.

Under the country's primary home healthcare system, nurses are only allowed to perform specialized services within the tightly limited scope of their professional areas of expertise. As a result, patients are often seen by 30 different healthcare professionals in the name of "administrative efficiency."

The Buurtzorg approach is radically different. In its system, small, highly trained teams of 10 to 12 nurses are given broad responsibility for the home care of 50 to 60 patients in a specific neighborhood. Under its more flexible approach, nurses assess patient needs, develop and implement plans, schedule medical visits, and provide needed and necessary services. This includes treatments such as dressing wounds, giving injections, assisting patients with baths and showers, and helping patients cope with dementia and end-of-life issues. Buurtzorg not only strives to maximize patient independence, but it also seeks to train family members and develop a network of needed community services.

The results have been impressive. Patient satisfaction has increased by 30 percent, the nurses are happier and more productive, and job turnover (relative to their peers who work in the existing system) is down significantly, because the nurses are less dissatisfied. Moreover, according to independent studies,[18] healthcare outcomes are better and costs are lower.

In other words, the Buurtzorg approach is a quintuple win for patients, families, nurses, community members, and taxpayers. Over the past 15 years, it has revolutionized home care in the Netherlands. It has now grown to include over 14,000 nurses and is responsible for serving over 100,000 citizens.

The significance of Buurtzorg's radical and holistic approach cannot be understated. It is true that under the existing system of measurement, the program is a success in that it saves the taxpayer money. But the success goes well beyond the economic value of the program. What of the value it has created for its patients in terms of independence? How does society put a price on that? How does it measure the peace of mind families have in knowing their loved ones are spending more time at home in close proximity to their friends and neighbors and not in hospitals?

Economic value is important, but it is not the only definition of success. Buurtzorg is an aspirational model of home healthcare that promises to grow into the future.

Reexamining the idea of what is normal, in 2021, Unilever decided to remove the word *normal* from all packaging and messaging on its 400-plus beauty and personal care products. The company announced it would also refrain from altering a model's shape, size, or skin color in all advertising campaigns and photo shoots.

Unilever recognizes that removing a single word is a mere stepping-stone, but it is a modest example of a company reexamining a

continued

long-held assumption. In Unilever's case, after surveying 10,000 people in Brazil, China, India, Indonesia, Nigeria, Saudi Arabia, South Africa, the United Kingdom, and the United States, it found that seven in ten people thought the word *normal* on beauty packaging to describe hair or skin had a negative impact by making most people feel excluded.[19]

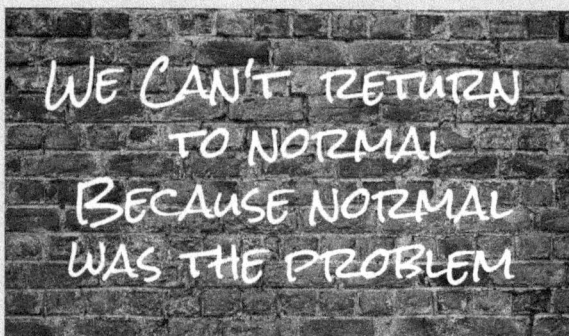

WE CAN'T RETURN TO NORMAL BECAUSE NORMAL WAS THE PROBLEM

The pandemic has changed many ideas of "normal" and has prompted questions of whether we want to return to what was considered normal. What is something "normal" that doesn't work for you? How might you, your company, or your organization reexamine your ideas about what is and what constitutes "normal"?

REEXAMINING SOCIAL WORK SOLUTIONS

Without knowing a ratchet from a wrench, Cathy Heying interrupted a successful 16-year career in social work to become an auto mechanic. She then opened her own auto repair shop.

Heying's unorthodox decision came after she had witnessed the downward-spiral impact that a costly or untimely car repair could have on the life of a person of limited means. All too often, the inability to afford a repair would lead to a devastating domino effect. Without a car, the person couldn't get to work, and this would often result in them losing their job. In turn, the lack of income would cause them to miss their rent, and, ultimately, they would be forced to move into a shelter or become homeless.

In 2008, at the age of 38, Heying entered a two-year program to become an auto mechanic, in a class filled with 18-year-old men. She graduated in 2010, and three years later, she opened The Lift Garage, an auto repair shop designed to help people whose income is below 150 percent of the federal poverty level affordably fix their cars. Unlike traditional repair shops that charge $100 an hour for labor and mark up all parts and equipment, The Lift Garage charges only $15 per hour for labor and provides all supplies at cost.[20]

Heying began her business with a single volunteer and operated only one day a week with a single repair bay. With the help of grants and donations, The Lift Garage is now open five days a week and has five full-time mechanics and operates five repair bays. Still, the demand is so great that there is currently a six-month backlog.

Since opening, Heying's business has completed over 3,000 repairs and helped stabilize the lives of over 1,500 individuals. In many ways, Heying is the epitome of the ethos of Generation Re. She has not only broken the vicious downward spiral for many people, but she has also replaced it with a virtuous cycle that has allowed people to live with dignity and better provide for themselves, their families, and their communities. It all began, however, with Heying reexamining the effectiveness of the social work in which she was engaged and finding another way to better serve people.

SKILLS AND INSIGHTS FOR REEXAMINING

"We would rather be ruined than changed.
We would rather die in our dread
Than climb the cross of the moment
And let our illusions die."

—W. H. AUDEN

In the following illustration, which middle line is longer, the top line or the bottom?

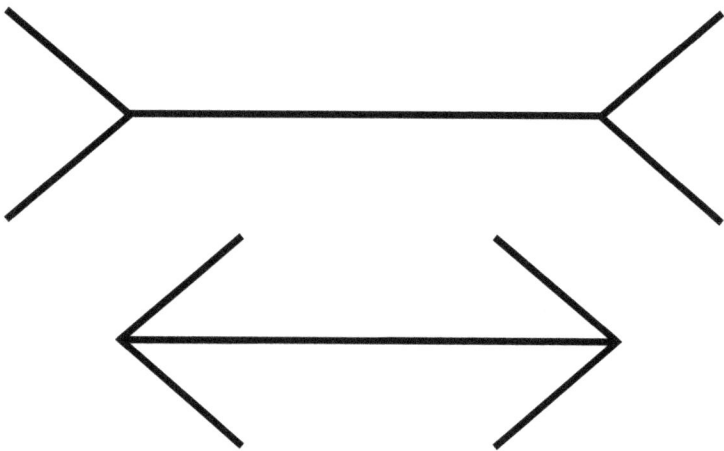

Both lines are the same size. (Feel free to reexamine them with a ruler.)

The visual, known as the Müller–Lyer illusion, serves as a playful reminder that the world is not always as it seems and that it is important to regularly reexamine those things we think are facts, immutable laws, and the truth. On reexamination, many are found to be illusions created by false assumptions and hidden biases.

While it is assuredly impossible to become completely unbiased in your thinking, it is possible to increase awareness of your biases. Undertaking this effort is an important place to begin reexamining.

As you ponder the three types of biases below, see if you can experience how each variation uniquely peels back the layers of assumption or habit. As you go deeper, it can be useful to consider the sources from which your biases grew.

Confirmation bias

This is one of today's most pervasive biases. It is human nature to surround ourselves with like-minded people, and in today's saturated 24/7 news cycle and powerful social media networks, we can get stuck in our own "echo chambers," hearing only from those who already share our existing beliefs. Concentrating on information that supports our existing biases to the disregard of contrary information can become habitual. Another trap of confirmation bias is interpreting information to support your existing beliefs.

One way to combat this bias is to assign more value to that information that challenges your viewpoint. For example, instead of listening to a well-known business commentator explain why stakeholder capitalism won't work, pay closer attention to someone not profiting from the existing system. Charlie Munger, Warren Buffet's lesser known but equally successful partner, has developed an iron-clad method for addressing this bias. He starts from the premise that having an opinion is not the same thing as forming an opinion and, of the two, the latter is more important. Therefore, Munger does not allow himself to hold an opinion on any topic or subject until he can recite the opposing viewpoint as well or better than his own arguments. It is a high standard to be sure, but it is one worth emulating.

"Opinion is really the lowest form of human knowledge. It requires no accountability, no understanding. The highest form of knowledge is empathy, for it requires us to suspend our egos and live in another's world."

—BILL BULLARD

Status quo bias

People tend to favor familiarity over the new. Today, it seems laughable that people once believed Earth was flat. Convincing them otherwise was, however, a long and hard-won battle. To overcome an attachment to the past that no longer serves us, it can help to reexamine a given issue by considering what's possible. For example, it may feel like humans are separate, independent entities, but, given the extraordinary advances in quantum physics pointing toward the objective reality of the interconnectedness of all things, is it not possible that, just as people now accept that Earth is round as a scientific fact, in the future, might people accept (and act upon) our interconnected-ness as a scientific fact?

Consider, for example, the emerging issue of legal rights for nature. Today, many people find the idea of granting legal person-hood to rivers, lakes, and mountains as an odd if not outlandish idea. But will it always be so? From New Zealand and India to communities in the United States, including Orlando, Florida, government and citizens have recently secured such rights for rivers. To challenge your bias, try to consider a given issue from a different perspective. Today, a number of non-sentient things, including corporations, ships, and municipal governments, are recognized as legal persons in judicial systems around the world. Is a river being considered a legal person any more absurd than a corporation such as Exxon being recognized as a legal person?

REEXAMINE SUCCESS

Have you ever wondered why so many people have lawns? If you think about it, humans are not born with an innate attraction to sizable patches of green grass. The history of the lawn may, however, provide some insight. During the medieval era, many feudal lords became wealthy enough that they could afford *not* to dedicate some of their land to growing crops. This uncultivated land became the spacious palatial grounds that many of us are familiar with today. Over time, people came to associate these spacious grounds as an indicator of affluence, and the lawn became an aspirational goal for many people. Over time, even though plot sizes became smaller, the lawn came to be synonymous with material success. If you currently have a lawn, you may want to reexamine its purpose and utility. In a growing number of communities people are now converting their lawns into carbon absorbing, pollinator-friendly gardens.

Implicit bias

Implicit bias is the collection of attitudes and stereotypes we have about people without our conscious awareness. Because we are not consciously aware of the bias, the decisions and actions we take based on our assumptions (rooted in the bias) do not register in our conscious mind as needing a second thought.

Simply becoming aware of the existence of implicit bias within ourselves is the first step toward addressing it. Questions are another helpful tool. Consider asking what you don't know. What aren't you seeing? In what ways is your experience limited in relationship to the subject? Can another person help you see the world in a new way?

Another tool for overcoming implicit bias in a business setting is to seek additive contribution. This requires questioning whether our criteria for decision-making will truly advance an issue or simply match the status quo. In hiring, for example, we tend to favor people who look like ourselves and who come from similar backgrounds. We must challenge this tendency, first through a regular practice of noticing our implicit biases and then by acting on the ever-widening worldview that can begin to emerge when our biases are challenged.

In the late 1950s, professional orchestras began placing curtains between conductors and those auditioning for the orchestra. The number of female musicians selected increased significantly after this change was institutionalized.

Today's employers might do something similar by redacting the names of universities or past employers from candidate resumes initiating the interview process. This would force them to focus on the skills of applicants and not rely on shortcuts, similarities, or other subjective inputs.

THE UPSIDE DOWN

"The absence of evidence is not evidence of absence."

—CARL SAGAN

The recent global pandemic has laid bare the truth that our view of reality is incomplete and, in many ways, upside down. It has highlighted the fact that essential workers, those who really make our world function, are not the well-compensated CEOs, the hedge fund managers, or the C-suite executives. They are the farmers, food production workers, truck drivers, grocery clerks, mail and delivery service workers, nurses, doctors, home health aides, long-term care providers, teachers, and others whose work makes possible every other form of work. Now is the time to reexamine the assumption that we can't create a world that allows each and every one of us an equal chance to flourish.

As Thomas Kuhn, the author of *The Structure of Scientific Revolutions*, said in his seminal work on paradigm shifts, "The [person] who embraces a new paradigm at an early stage must often do so in defiance of the evidence provided by problem-solving. He must, that is, have faith that the new paradigm will succeed with the many large problems that confront it, knowing only that the older paradigm has failed with a few. A decision of that kind can only be made on faith."[21]

There is much in this world that needs to be reexamined—our stewardship of the planet, homelessness, poverty, income inequality—and we need more exemplars who see with new eyes and hear with new ears. We need people freed from the distortions of social and cultural bias, who act on behalf of all people, not just a select few. In time, growing legions of Generation Re will reimagine and redesign a world where every individual and company will compete not to be the best *in* the world but to be the best *for* the world.

As you take these steps to increase awareness of your own biases, a more meaningful, revitalizing interaction with the world awaits you.

Try this: In the space below, draw a tree. You need not be a skilled artisan, and you can draw any tree you wish. Sketch as many details as possible in five minutes—trunk, branches, bark, leaves, and so forth. Do not turn the page before completing this task.

Did you draw the roots of the tree? Approximately 90 percent of people leave out this critical element, even though they were asked to draw as many details as possible. Roots, of course, are essential to the health, growth, life, and regenerative capacity of any tree.

This exercise serves as a reminder that it can be difficult to see what we can't see. But if we are to expand our sense of the rich possibilities that the future can hold, it is important to comprehend the ways in which we don't always see the world as clearly or completely as we like to believe we do.

Chapter 4

REFRAME

*"Reframing requires asking 'What if' and
'How about' even when things are going very well."*

—THE INNOVATIVE MINDSET,
BRAVE NEW WORKSHOP

In his classic 1884 book, *Flatland: A Romance of Many Dimensions*, author Edwin Abbott invites readers into the two-dimensional world of Flatland. The story's narrator, A Square, begins by explaining that Flatland is like a sheet of paper in that it only consists of length and width. There is no such thing as height. It is a universe where its inhabitants can move right and left and back and forth but not up and down.

In a series of dreams, A Square travels to Lineland, a one-dimensional universe where the inhabitants perceive themselves as lines and can only move right or left. A Square also visits Pointland, a land with no dimensions in which the inhabitants can only perceive themselves because they can't move anywhere else. A Square ridicules these inhabitants because, in spite of his best efforts, he can't convince them of his two-dimensional reality.

In a third dream, A Square is visited by Sphere, an inhabitant of a three-dimensional world, who confronts him with the gospel of the third dimension. It is now *his* turn to struggle with the existence of a dimension beyond his comprehension. It takes some time, but A Square comes to accept a different reality, because he was able to recall his own challenge of convincing the inhabitants of the one- and no-dimension universes to see the world from a different perspective.

In an imaginative leap, A Square then challenges Sphere to entertain the idea of a four-dimensional world and even the possibility of multidimensional worlds, but he is shocked when Sphere can't entertain such notions.

The point of the novella is to make the reader aware that what they perceive as "real" is entirely dependent on the dimensions that they currently inhabit, such as social, cultural, linguistic, or other constructed realities. Abbott used a fictional account to reframe people's perspective of their existing reality as a way to stay open to new possibilities. His broader point was that, when we gain new perspectives, we move closer to new and deeper truths about our world—and ourselves.

FROM EXTERNAL FOCUS TO INTERNAL REFRAMING

Here's a light story to further introduce the notion of reframing. A meticulous homeowner had grown exasperated with his inability to control dandelions in his yard. At his wit's end, the man consulted a master gardener.

"I hate the pesky weed and need your help," he pleaded.

The master gardener ran through a litany of options.

"I have tried all of those things," the man said, "and they haven't worked!"

The gardener reflected for a moment before replying, "Well, then, I suggest you learn to love dandelions."

The gardener's words capture the wisdom of Ralph Waldo Emerson, who once said a weed is just "a plant whose virtues have not yet been discovered." It also serves as a powerful example of reframing.

Rather than trying to alter your existing reality (e.g., getting rid of dandelions), it is often easier and more fruitful to reframe your internal view of things (e.g., love dandelions). Can you think of an issue or situation in your work or personal life that could use reframing in this way?

Greta Thunberg: Climate change to climate crisis

On August 20, 2018, a small, shy 15-year-old girl, dressed in a blue hoodie, engaged in a modest act of teen rebellion by skipping school and holding a hand-drawn sign outside the Swedish Parliament. The poster read, "*Skolstrejk for Klimatat*," or "School strike for climate." It was the ninth grader's way of calling attention to her government's lack of action in meeting the goals it had set as a signatory of the 2015 Paris Agreement on climate change. No one paid much attention to her solitary protest.

The next week, a single climate activist joined the young woman's cause in protest. The following week, the number grew to four and then eight. In time, hundreds and then thousands and, ultimately, millions of people from all over the world joined Greta

Thunberg in protesting the lack of governmental attention to and action on the climate crisis. In so doing, legions of supporters and fellow activists have lifted and amplified her once humble voice into a powerful force for change.

Before millions joined her, Thunberg was working to reframe the issue of climate change. Her first effort occurred in Davos in February 2019, when, as a relative unknown, she was invited to the World Economic Forum to address the world's most powerful corporate and political leaders. She took to the stage and bluntly declared to the global elite sitting before her, "We are in the beginning of a mass extinction, and all you can talk about is money and fairy tales of eternal growth." Later in the same speech, Thunberg was even more direct: "For way too long, the politicians and the people in power have gotten away with not doing anything at all to fight the climate crisis and the ecological crisis, but we will make sure that you do not get away with it any longer." She then concluded with these poignant words: "I want you to panic. I want you to feel the fear I feel every day. And then I want you to do something about it."[1]

The video footage of her candid and uncompromising speech went viral, and with it, three decades of dry debates and complicated discussion over parts per million and acceptable degrees of warming began to give way. Thunberg had successfully reframed the debate from "climate change" to "climate crisis" by emphasizing that it was no longer a scientific and technical matter requiring further study but, rather, a dire situation that demanded immediate action.

When Thunberg addresses groups, she pulls no punches. She speaks in short, direct, unflinching, and uncomplicated sentences: *The ocean will rise, cities will flood, and hundreds of millions will suffer from drought and extreme poverty.* It is this authenticity that has cut through the fog of confusion cloaking the climate crisis and focused people on the urgency of taking action.

Thunberg, though, was just getting started. Her rising global profile garnered her a speaking slot at the United Nations' 2019 Climate Action Summit and, only 13 months from that August day when she stood alone outside the Swedish House of Parliament, Thunberg again took to the podium. Sporting her signature braids, Thunberg delivered a scathing condemnation to a full assembly of the world's leaders: "You are failing us."[2]

In the same speech, she stared down her audience and said, "How dare you? You have stolen my dreams and my childhood." She further reframed the climate debate by humanizing the climate crisis as a matter of generational injustice.

Two months later, Thunberg even confronted would-be supporters, allies, and environmental activists at the UN Climate Change Conference in Warsaw, Poland, saying, "You say you love your children above all else, and yet you are stealing their future in front of their eyes."[3]

And herein lies the real strength of Thunberg's reframing. By speaking in terms of dreams and childhoods and love, she connects with people's hearts. She does not, however, stop there. She refuses to allow people off the hook and confronts them directly, addressing their hypocrisy and their inaction. This combination of generational injustice and a call to responsibility is producing real results. The cognitive dissonance between her audience's genuine feelings for their children and their own lack of action will, at some point, become too great for them, and they will finally be moved to take meaningful action.

Thunberg's reframing has resulted in tangible results. In addition to mobilizing 4 million activists to participate in Friday for the Future strikes around the world, her words have caused large corporations and governments to begin to modify their behavior in tangible ways. Since her address, the United Kingdom, France, and Germany have passed legislation agreeing to eliminate their carbon footprint by 2050. Amazon, spurred into action by 4,200 of its employees who joined the massive global strike and demanded the company to do more on behalf of the environment, has created a $2 billion fund to invest in companies and technologies designed to decarbonize the economy and protect the planet.[4]

Other companies, including Google, Microsoft, and Twitter, have taken similar—albeit smaller—measures. Moreover, Thunberg's refusal to fly to the UN summit over concern about the amount of carbon her flight would have emitted (she chose instead to sail to New York City) was instrumental in getting KLM, one of the world's largest airlines, to voluntarily introduce a "Fly responsibly" campaign that encouraged people not to fly for nonessential travel.[5]

By walking the talk, Thunberg has inspired the creation of a new word, *flygskam*. While literally translated as "flight shaming," the term is aimed at convincing travelers to choose more eco-friendly means of transportation. The concept so pierced the public's consciousness that, even before the pandemic, it was responsible for reducing air traffic in Germany by 12 percent.[6]

Part of what makes Greta Thunberg's story so powerful is that she was not the first person to protest on behalf of climate change. She wasn't famous, she didn't come from money or fame, and she didn't have the gravitas of a politician or the pedigree of a scientist. She was just an ordinary teenager who was willing to follow her heart and consciousness and speak up and act. In doing so, Thunberg's voice has served as a moral clarion call and given voice to an entire generation. Together, these voices have created a global attitudinal shift that is having a measurable impact.

Thread International: From intersecting crises to integrated opportunity

In 2010, in the wake of the devastating earthquake in Haiti, Ian Rosenberger traveled to Port-au-Prince with a plan to take and sell photos to contribute to the relief cause. While he was there, he met Tassy, a young man with a large facial tumor, and Rosenberger's mission shifted. He raised the funds to fly Tassy to the United States to have the tumor removed and his face reconstructed.

When the time came to return Tassy to Haiti, Rosenberger realized that his efforts to help the young man would be little more than an exercise in self-congratulation if he simply left him in a city filled with trash and mired in poverty. Rosenberger then asked himself a powerful question: What would it mean for Tassy to not need him anymore?

The question prompted a good deal of thinking and soul-searching that led to three insights. First, Rosenberger came to understand he needed to shift his focus from one of *helping* Tassy and others in Haiti to one of working to solve the systemic issues underlying the country's pervasive joblessness and poverty. This led to the second insight: that poverty isn't just the absence of money; it is also the absence of dignity. The third insight was that doing good in the world and doing well in business were not mutually exclusive ideas. He saw a way to use one of Haiti's larger problems—plastic waste—to help address its biggest problem—poverty.

Rosenberger reframed problems into opportunities and created Thread International, a company that collects plastic bottles and trash in Haiti—and now in Honduras and Taiwan. The company then converts it into yarns and fabrics and sells the sustainable material to apparel companies around the world.

In the process, Thread International (which has been split into two separate companies but remains a for-profit company) has created a triple win situation by ridding Haiti's ocean waters and landfills of more than 30 million plastic bottles, creating thousands of jobs, and keeping the operation financially sustainable through a smart business model. Moreover, the jobs address multidimensional poverty by providing workers with fair wages and upward mobility through educational opportunities, job training, and healthcare. The jobs also inspire dignity by furnishing the workers with the knowledge that, by supplying the most responsible fabric on the planet to a number of leading global brands, including Timberlake, Reebok, Kenneth Cole, and Under Armour. They are an integral component in the emerging circular economy that supports planetary sustainability.

Harvard Medical School and InterMountain Health: From illness to holistic wellness

"When I is replaced with we, *even illness becomes wellness."*
—CHARLES ROPPEL

Harvard Medical School's old statement read as follows: "To create and nurture a diverse community of the best people committed to leadership in alleviating human suffering caused by disease."

Today, the new statement, drafted in 2018, reads, "To nurture a diverse, inclusive community dedicated to alleviating suffering and improving health and well-being for all through excellence in teaching and learning, discovery and scholarship, and service and leadership."[7]

The words *and improving health and well-being for all* may not seem profound, but, as one healthcare commentator said, it was "bold and visionary."[8] The reason is twofold. First, the old language assumes a present problem ("suffering") and that it takes the "best people" (i.e., experts) to solve that problem.

The new statement no longer accepts as a given that healthcare can only be defined as the lessening of a disease or physical ailment. It instead broadens healthcare to include a community-based mission of pursuing health for everyone.

In this more expansive pursuit, a subtle, unseen, and underappreciated shift has taken place. Health and healthcare are becoming more humanized. The focus has moved from an administrative emphasis on reducing costs, increasing efficiency, and alleviating suffering to a more radical shift of doing the right thing by focusing on outcomes people truly care about—namely, staying healthy in the first place. Patients are no longer limited to following the orders of the "best people." They are empowered to take responsibility for their own health and wellness by exercising more, eating healthier, tracking their sleep, and monitoring their general well-being.

A second example comes from Intermountain Healthcare, a not-for-profit healthcare system offering hospital and other medical services in the western part of the United States. Similar to Harvard Medical School, Intermountain reframed its business by breaking healthcare into two separate parts: health and care.

On the care side of its business are the activities of what is traditionally considered the work of a hospital: handling emergencies; offering beds, surgical suites, and intensive care units; and providing patients access to world-class specialists.

Its health business is where reframing is ushering in a new model. By sending nurses out into the community to do home assessments, Intermountain Healthcare is engaging in more proactive and preventive care. It is focusing on preventing accidents. For example, nurses routinely inspect the homes of elderly people for loose carpets and poor lighting that may lead to falls. It is also addressing substance abuse and generally tending to issues that will keep people *out* of the hospital. Where appropriate, Intermountain is also working in partnership with families and civic and religious organizations to achieve these outcomes.

Reframing has allowed both Harvard Medical School and Intermountain Healthcare to address the reality that much of what truly matters to people happens *in between* the visits to a doctor's office or a hospital. It's as much about food, transportation, housing, and creating a safe and nurturing environment as it is about the delivery of specific medical services.

In the coming years, as technological advances in mobile communication, artificial intelligence, big data, the Internet of Things and smart sensors, genomics, wearables, blockchain, virtual and augmented reality, 5G, bio- and nanotechnology, and telemedicine continue to accelerate, scores of businesses will leverage these new tools to take this more human-focused approach to care to new levels. They will allow people to better monitor, track, and take care of their own health. A new paradigm of healthcare is emerging, but it first had to be reframed.

REFRAMING THE NARRATIVE: TURNING THE DARKEST HOUR INTO THE FINEST HOUR

In June 1940, 338,000 British soldiers were pinned down in northern France, at Dunkirk. Great Britain was not only facing an extraordinary loss of human life in the face of the advancing German army, but it was also in danger of suffering a deflating retreat that threatened to destroy the country's morale and, along with it, the nation's resistance to confronting Hitler's totalitarian regime.

Newly appointed prime minister Winston Churchill took to the radio and, in one of the twentieth century's more powerful addresses, reframed the narrative of Dunkirk from one of humiliation and retreat to a rousing call of arms. In the speech, Churchill resolved that the country's citizens "shall go on to the end. We shall defend our island, whatever the cost may be; we shall fight on the beaches; we shall fight on the landing grounds; we shall fight in the fields and in the streets; we shall fight in the hills; we shall never surrender."[9] Spurred to action, some 900 civilian vessels sailed from England and ferried nearly all of the 338,000 soldiers safely back home.

Churchill wasn't done, though. By any objective measure, Dunkirk was a colossal defeat for England, but that was not how the prime minister portrayed the country's darkest hour. He reframed it. In a memorable line, from another radio address, Churchill thundered, "If the British Empire and its Commonwealth last a thousand years, men will still say, 'This was their finest hour.'"

Few leaders will be presented with as horrific a challenge as Churchill faced in the spring of 1940, but dark hours always loom, and a leader's ability to reframe perspectives can steer a dire situation toward an ultimate win.

SKILLS AND INSIGHTS FOR REFRAMING

*"If a problem can't be solved within the frame it was conceived,
the solution lies in reframing the problem."*

—BRIAN MCGREEVY

Imagine owning an old, large, multistory apartment complex. The elevators, which have been operational since the building was constructed a hundred years ago, begin to slow down. This draws the ire of many tenants, who are increasingly frustrated by the longer-than-usual wait times, especially during the peak-use hours of morning and afternoon. In time, the complaints multiply, and a number of occupants threaten to break their lease and move out of the building unless the problem is resolved.

Imagine further that, upon investigation, none of the options a team of engineers recommend to fix the problem, including upgrading the motor, installing a new, lighter elevator, or investing in advanced software and algorithms, are economically viable. After exhausting all options, the lead engineer announces that, short of people willing to adhere to a regimented schedule of when they can leave and return to their apartments, nothing can be done. The residents will simply have to live with the problem, and management will simply have to accept some loss of tenants.

The problem, as described, was a real problem many building owners encountered years ago. Contrary to the lead engineer's suggestion, a solution did exist, but it first required someone to reframe the problem.

According to the story, the desperate manager called a team meeting and explained the problem to his staff. Everyone sided with the engineers, except for a young, recently hired staffer. This worker happened to hold a degree in psychology, and, instead of focusing on elevator performance, he asked a different question: Why were tenants complaining about waiting only a few minutes?

After some investigation, it was discovered that most of the complaints were the result of boredom. Armed with this insight, the young man suggested installing mirrors in the boarding areas and in the lobby. The manager took the employee's suggestion, and the number of complaints dropped immediately—to nearly zero. The tactic worked because most people enjoy looking at themselves in the mirror and tend to lose track of time when distracted.

What makes the story interesting is that the solution doesn't address the stated problem. It doesn't make the elevator move any faster. Instead, the employee reframed the issue and, in the process, proposed a different understanding of the problem. His insight was that the underlying issue was behavioral and not situational. Today, in most buildings, it is now common to find mirrors in the lobby areas. It is a low-cost solution to a widespread problem.

The story serves as a reminder that, sometimes, creative and innovative solutions to problems come from finding and developing alternative definitions of the problem. In a world where perception is deemed reality, the following insightful narratives may stimulate shifts in perspective that can, in turn, help you shape new definitions of your own persistent problems.

The good of the many over the good of the few

In 1884, Auguste Rodin was commissioned by the French port city of Calais to create a sculpture commemorating an event during the Hundred Years' War (1337–1453). After laying siege to the city for 11 months, the king of England agreed to spare the starving citizens of Calais if the city's six leaders would surrender themselves for execution.

When Rodin completed *The Burghers of Calais* (see figure 4.1) in 1889, it was met with widespread disapproval. Instead of placing the heroes on a pedestal, the common practice, Rodin placed the burghers on ground level, with looks of great anguish etched into their bodies and onto their faces. It was Rodin's goal to reframe heroes as people who make difficult decisions *in spite* of their fears. In this way, Rodin was also attempting to reframe hero status away from something akin to worship and into an aspiration anyone in the community could live up to.

Figure 4.1. The Burghers of Calais *by Rodin.*

It is not known whether Rodin was consciously trying to get the citizens of Calais to embrace the difficulty of setting aside personal interest for the benefit of the broader community; nevertheless, this story offers a rather extreme illustration of an outlook that prioritizes the good of the many over the good of the few.

A question of focus

Figure 4.2. A tiger and a jungle.

What do you see in figure 4.2? If this image is shown to people in the West, the most common answer is "a tiger in a jungle." If the same picture is shown to people in the East, the most common answer is "a jungle with a tiger in it." The latter point of view emphasizes the big picture, or the community first and the individual second. This shift in perspective is a key factor in the ethos of Generation Re.

Such a shift in perspective might manifest in the form of a business like Tentree, a Canadian apparel company that plants 10 trees for every item purchased.[10] The company does this because it wants to help rebuild local communities in Cambodia, Canada, Haiti, Indonesia, Madagascar, Senegal, and the United States around sustainable industries such as forestry. In other words, Tentree does not so much see itself as an individual business operating within different communities as it sees itself as integrated within the broader community.

Enough!

> *"He who knows that enough is enough*
> *will always have enough."*
>
> —LAO TZU

The previous quote is attributed to Lao Tzu, the sixth-century Chinese author of *Tao Te Ching* and a leading figure in Taoism. The concept of enough is also beautifully captured in the Swedish word *lagom* (pronounced LAH-gum), which means "just right."

The common legend is that the word comes from the phrase *laget om*, which means "around the whole team" and which dates back to the Viking era, when communal horns of fermented honey wine were passed around the ship. Everyone had to sip their share and not a bit more.[11] As one might imagine, a ship where only a few Vikings were hydrated and the remainder were parched would not have been a conducive strategy for long-term success.

Today, *lagom* captures the zeitgeist of a handful of emerging trends. In the field of economics, for example, a growing number of economists, politicians, and citizens are reframing the current economic paradigm away from the idea that more is better and that unlimited growth is an unmitigated good. Others are seeking to maximize societal well-being by minimizing consumption—for example, by living in smaller, even tiny, houses, sharing items instead of purchasing them outright, and generally seeking to strike a healthier balance between needs and wants.

In a society where Big Gulps, mega mansions, and all-you-can-eat buffets are still common, *lagom* strikes at the heart of three toxic contemporary myths: There's not enough (scarcity). More is better (greed). And That's just the way it is (complacency).

"JOE HELLER"
Kurt Vonnegut

True story, Word of Honor:
Joseph Heller, an important and funny writer
now dead,
and I were at a party given by a billionaire
on Shelter Island.
I said, "Joe, how does it make you feel
to know that our host only yesterday
may have made more money
than your novel 'Catch-22'
has earned in its entire history?"
And Joe said, "I've got something he can never have."
And I said, "What on earth could that be, Joe?"
And Joe said, "The knowledge that I've got enough."
Not bad! Rest in peace!

Via negativa

Via negativa is a Latin-derived phrase meaning to "describe something by saying what it is not." While the phrase originates from Christian theology, it can have multiple applications, including as a strategy for reframing business issues.

A business, for example, might think about the type of culture it wants to create by asking what type of management practices it most wants to *avoid*. For example, this reframing might effectively bring to light those practices that inhibit rather than support an employee initiative, or practices that create barriers to employees finding meaning in their work.

From a personal perspective, via negativa asks what kind of person or leader you *don't* want to be. Few people are inclined to say that they want to be arrogant, overly confident, or bad listeners, but these potential weaknesses can often more easily be exposed by intentionally identifying them.

It has been said that chess grandmasters win by *not losing*, and in business, as in life, stripping away bad habits frequently yields the greatest success. A powerful technique (which has incorrectly been attributed to Warren Buffett, but which is still useful in helping people reframe their personal goals) is this: People are encouraged to draw up a list of their top 25 life goals and then are asked to prioritize them in order from 1 to 25. When this task is complete, they are to circle their top five goals. They are also told to circle the bottom 20. The first five, of course, become the person's to-do list. The bottom 20, however, become their avoid-at-all-costs list. This reframing shocks and surprises a lot of people (after all, there are so many worthy and important things on the list), but the point is this: In order for people to achieve the goals they consider most important in their life, they must let go of some other very good things so those things do not become a distraction to achieving what matters most.

Focused questions

"It's not the answer that enlightens but the question."

—EUGENE IONESCO

A wealthy man announced to his community that he was giving away all of his worldly possessions. As we would expect, people came from near and far to claim whatever bounty they could. True to his word, the man gave away everything he owned.

Later in the evening, a straggler who had traveled a great distance approached the man. The man looked at him and said, "I am sorry, but you are late. I have already given everything away."

The straggler replied, "Oh, I did not come for any of your possessions. I came to know how you were able to give everything away."

Now, that is a powerful question—the kind that can reframe and reinvent a life. Reframing by using questions need not be so profound. Consider this question, a version of which many of us have been asked throughout our lives: How creative are you? (If you are so inclined, on a scale of 1 to 10, give yourself an answer.) Now, using the exact same four words, can we ask a more useful question?

How about, instead of "How *creative* are you?" you ask, "How are *you* creative?" The former requires a judgment-based response, whereas the latter captures a deeper truth: We are each creative in our own unique way.

Two individuals who have asked better questions are Sam Polk and David Foster, the founders of Everytable, a restaurant dedicated to serving healthy food in lower-income neighborhoods of Los Angeles. To paraphrase, the pair used two questions to reframe their idea about what a restaurant could do: *How can we leverage economic power for people at the bottom of the pyramid? Can we charge different customers in different communities different prices for the same product in order to increase the distribution of healthy food?* As a result, they concluded that price could be used not to maximize profits but to better serve the disadvantaged. Everytable uses variable pricing to charge people in affluent neighborhoods more money so they can charge customers in the lower-income food desert areas of inner Los Angeles *less* money in order that they too can have access to fresh, healthy, organic food.

Here are a few other reframing questions:

- What if our goal isn't short-term success but, rather, long-term sustainability?

- How can work be a place where you *find* yourself instead of losing yourself?

- What if a business's goal isn't simply to grow larger and more profitable but to increase the overall ability for all people to thrive in each community it touches?

Time in terms of future generations

All too often, business leaders focus on matters in the following order: short term, midterm, and long term. Put another way, the order looks like this: now, next, future. Now consider this order:

now, future, next. The value of reframing the order is that the future can, should, and does influence your next step. An essential task for Generation Re is to reframe time, extending your sense of it beyond individual life span to include future generations.

Management consultant John Hagel has created a strategy he calls the *zoom out, zoom in* approach that helps businesses reframe strategy and tactics. Zooming out may feel less comfortable for business leaders, because it requires consideration of a variety of factors that could influence the future, including the accelerating pace of technological change, changing demographics, evolving customer preferences and tastes, and a myriad of other social, political, and cultural shifts. Nevertheless, with study, research, trend forecasting, and the assistance of outside experts, futurists, and provocateurs, it is possible to gain a general sense of what business must be doing today in order to position itself for the emerging future.

Hagel recommends beginning the zoom out process by answering these two questions:

- What will our relevant market look like 10–20 years from now?

- What kind of company will we need to be 10–20 years from now to be successful in that market?

Once the future trends have been identified and the questions have been answered, it is then possible to zoom in and identify two or three initiatives that the organization could pursue in the middle term (6–12 months) that would have the greatest impact on accelerating movement toward the desired future.

QUICK REFRAMING TECHNIQUE

The Long Now Foundation has created an innovative way to reframe time and foster longer-term thinking. It has created a 10,000 year clock.[12] Today, most of us think of the calendar year as having four digits (2021, 2022, 2030, 2050, 2100, etc.), but employing five digits and placing a zero at the beginning of the year so that the years now read 02020, 02022, 02030, 02050, and 02100, and so forth creates a subtle but powerful shift in perspective. Like an odometer far from reaching 100,000 miles, the Long Now Foundation's method emphasizes how much time lies ahead instead of only focusing on the current time.

It is a simple reframing technique, but it holds the potential to help people rethink their assumptions about time. Suddenly, the present year is but a fraction of time into a much longer-term future. As a result, people and organizations are stretched to think beyond the next day, week, quarter, or year—even the next generation—and into a deeper, longer future. The expectation is that this new way of seeing will lead to actions that better reflect society's responsibilities to future generations.

Reframing love

Love is arguably the most important aspect of life yet one that we often see only from a limited perspective. It is not a word most businesspeople are comfortable using, but if business is to play a vital role in helping bring about a reunion of mind, heart, and spirit, its leaders could benefit from pondering its multiple meanings.

The ancient Greeks had six separate words for love. Eros, most commonly defined as romantic love, may be the most familiar, and this is where the West centers much of its attention. There is, of course, nothing wrong with *eros*, but its overemphasis can inhibit business leaders from considering how other definitions of love, such as *philia* (friendship love) and *agape* (a general empathy or loving kindness for all people), can be boldly integrated into business leadership principles.

Philia and agape are notions that can facilitate expressions of love for employees, customers, and the planet without coming across as too "soft." For example, Brian Chesky, the CEO of Airbnb, had the concept of agape in his mind and heart when he had to make the very painful decision to lay off some of his employees in the early days of the pandemic. He said, "I have a deep feeling of love for all of you."[13] His love was then manifested in a series of heartfelt actions, including directing his entire human resources staff's attention to helping their laid-off colleagues find new gainful employment.

VIEWING FROM EVERY ANGLE

Unlike the common experience in Western society of viewing paintings from a fixed, individual perspective, as they hang on a wall, Australian Aboriginal people place paintings on the ground, sit in a circle around the painting, and ask each member of the tribal community to describe it from their perspective.[14] Beyond the novel awareness that this practice inspires for us in the West, honoring all perspectives through collectively viewing art from every angle is a beautiful metaphor that encompasses the notions of reuniting, reimagining, and reframing. That is to say, the world of tomorrow has not yet been painted, and successfully creating a future world that will work for everyone rests on the inclusion of perspectives from the multiplicity of human voices.

Is this more challenging than a leader–follower model? Yes. More time consuming? Probably. But hearing all stakeholder voices will go a long way toward transforming more narrowly conceived notions of business problems into innovative, dynamic, and empowering visions that more than make up for these challenges through the long-term viability of its resulting solutions, which promise to build a better future *for all.*

Chapter 5

REDESIGN

"Design creates culture. Culture shapes values.
Values determine the future."

—ROBERT L. PETERS

I n the fall of 2014, Sophie Windsor Clive and Liberty Smith were canoeing on the River Shannon, in Ireland, when they captured an amazingly elaborate and acrobatic display of thousands of starlings swooping and diving in perfect synchrony. It was as though the birds were connected as one in an ever-changing pattern. This natural phenomenon is known as a *murmuration.*

Although much still remains unknown about the beautiful dynamic, it is believed that murmurations were born of evolutionary pressures designed to help starlings find new sources of food and avoid predators. The technique is beneficial and perhaps even instrumental in the starlings' long-term survival.

When the thousands of individual starlings coalesce, a murmuration can almost be considered a phase transition (defined—within a system—as on the edge of transformation), such as when water turns to ice or a liquid turns into a gas. In this sense, murmurations serve as the perfect metaphor for redesign. If humans are to survive as a species, we would be wise to use evolutionary pressures like climate change to channel our collective ingenuity to transition away from our fierce grip on individualism, separation, and independence and toward something more akin to a fluid, cohesive, and interdependent whole.

It may be difficult to imagine a large group of humans moving with the speed, synchronization, and perfection of a murmuration, but years ago Craig Reynolds created a computer simulation of a murmuration in which he coded the actions of every bird.[1] The result was a choppy, inefficient, and unintelligent murmuration. But when each bird in the simulation was given three simple principles to follow, the result was fluid, efficient, and intelligent. Reynolds's research suggests that self-organizing complexity is possible, although it is unlikely to be born from strict command-and-control systems, long-range guidance, or complex regulatory governance structures. Instead, it appears that self-organizing complexity might be best achieved by following a few basic rules.

In the case of the starlings, the birds perform their wonderfully complex dance without bumping into one another by following three rules: First, every starling in the flock interacts with only the six or seven starlings in its immediate vicinity. Next, the birds match the speed and direction of their closest neighbors. And, third, any bird that has become separated moves back in the direction of the flock. Once it has rejoined the others, it adheres to the first two rules.

If modern society is to flourish into the future, it seems clear that new guidelines are necessary. Fortunately, members of Generation Re are creating a new set of rules, and from their example could arise the more fluid, well-functioning society of our imaginations.

HOW WOLVES CHANGE RIVERS

"The change of perception of ourselves and the human species in relationship to the rest of the natural world . . . has the potential of provoking a fundamental change in worldview and therefore design practice—a shift from design for humans but against nature to a design approach that recognizes that humanity is a codependent part of nature. In recognizing that life is fundamentally cooperative and symbiotic, designers can shift towards a symbiotic, synergistic or win–win approach to design that integrates humanity into natural processes."

—DANIEL CHRISTIAN WAHL, "Design for Human and Planetary Health" (2006)

In 1995, gray wolves were reintroduced into Yellowstone National Park 70 years after being driven away by farmers, ranchers, trappers, and hunters. The impact of the wolves' return was startling. Immediately, the herds of elk, which had grown accustomed to grazing the land and trees since the wolves' disappearance, began to thin. More important, though, was how the wolves altered the behavior of the elk, who began to avoid low-level valleys, meadows, and gorges, where they could more easily be trapped and preyed on by wolf packs. Because elk are herbivores, this allowed willows, aspens, and cottonwood trees to reestablish in these low-lying areas. In six years, some trees quintupled in size.

The reemergent forests not only brought birds and insects back, but they also provided food and shelter for a rich assortment of other plants and animals, including beavers. Like wolves, beavers are engineers of the ecosystem, and the dams they built created additional ecosystems for otters, muskrats, ducks, fish, and reptiles. The wolves, because they also worked to control the number of coyotes, helped rabbits and mice—the natural prey of coyotes—to return to the park. These animals, in turn, brought hawks and eagles back as well as weasels, foxes, and badgers. Even bears, which could now find berries on trees (as well as feed on the carrion of the wolves), grew in number.

What was truly remarkable, however, was how the wolves affected the flow of rivers. Due to the newly reestablished abundance of trees along the riverbanks, soil erosion diminished, allowing the riverbanks to stabilize, deeper channels to form, and the rivers to forge a straighter path.

Although they were small in number—only 41 wolves were reintroduced in 1995—their impact was transformative.[2] They helped create lush, regenerating forests that now support a rich, thriving, and biologically diverse ecosystem.

The metaphor of the murmuration reminds us that complex yet fluid interconnectivity can arise from a few guiding rules, and the story of the reintroduction of the wolves illustrates how small changes can have far-reaching, regenerative repercussions. We'll now introduce you to a cutting-edge economist, a progressive city, a political reformer, and a handful of businesses and innovators working to create these new rules and to transform the world into a healthier, regenerative future.

DOUGHNUT ECONOMICS

"We live in a society, not an economy."

—UNKNOWN

It goes without saying that the task of redesigning the global economy is complex. Countless books have been written on the topic, involving diverse schools of economic thought, and entire political ideologies have sought to tackle the issue. Some of these have contributed materially to the improvement of society and the well-being of countless individuals, but they all have fallen short in significant ways.

If a picture is worth a thousand words, the shortcomings of today's system of capitalism are captured in the following photo.

Figure 5.1.

We can all agree that no one, especially a child as young as the one in the photo, should have to tease out a miserable

existence amid stifling heat, a growing pile of filth and trash, and a diminishing supply of fresh, clean water. Moreover, it is inconceivable that the planet can sustain the level of environmental abuse and degradation in this photo. Sadly, photos similar to this one, and even worse, could be captured from numerous places on our planet.

The challenge of our times is to create an economic system capable of pulling out that young child (and the estimated 700 million more like him[3]) from wretched poverty without inflicting further damage to the environment. It is an enormously complicated task and, fortunately, Kate Raworth, an economist at Oxford University, has stepped up to the challenge. Raworth has created a new economic paradigm dubbed *doughnut economics*.[4]

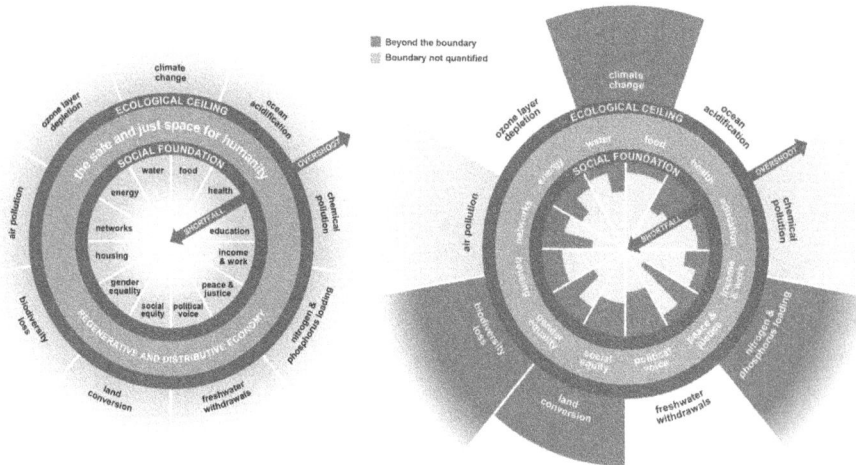

Figures 5.2 and 5.3. Doughnut economics.
The Doughnut of social and planetary boundaries.

On the inside of the green ring of Raworth's doughnut are the basic necessities essential to the survival of individuals and societies—water, food, energy, healthcare, housing, education, income, work, and social equity. The goal is to lift up the hundreds of millions of people living below the social foundation into the green, thriving area of the doughnut.

At the outer edge of the doughnut are the planetary constraints that society must operate within if it is to continue to flourish and prosper into the long-term future. Specifically, a healthy economic system cannot do excessive damage to the climate; acidify our oceans; remove too many forests; pollute the air; overfertilize farmlands; withdraw too much fresh water from our lakes, streams, and rivers; or create further biodiversity loss.

In the middle space, between the inner and outer rings, lies a sweet spot. Raworth labels this "the safe and just space for humanity"—that is, the space where the basic needs of all of the planet's inhabitants are met within the ecological limits of what Earth can sustain.

Raworth's redesign process consists of seven steps:

Change the goal

For the better part of the last century, the goal of economic progress has been measured by gross domestic product. Society can no longer accept a system that perpetuates growth for growth's sake; rather, it needs a system that thrives regardless of whether it grows.

See the big picture

It is now understood that the economy is wholly embedded within nature. No longer can the planet's resources be overlooked and viewed as unlimited.

Nurture human nature

Humans are not the self-interested, calculating unflinchingly rational individuals that modern economics has based its models on. Instead, people are social, interdependent, and more emotion-driven than we tend to believe, and the field of economics must take this understanding into consideration.

Get savvy with the system

The economy is not a Newtonian machine consisting only of the fixed variables of labor and income, savings and investment, taxes and spending, and imports and exports. Instead, it is a complex and ever-evolving system and needs to be treated as such.

Design to distribute

An unequal system is a choice, not a given. In this sense, inequality is a design failure. Nature offers no example whereby a tiny minority of the population reaps, consumes, and hordes a vast majority of the existing resources. New ways to redistribute wealth exist, and they can and must be designed and nurtured.

Create to regenerate

The old linear system of inputting resources and then spewing out waste is not sustainable. Instead, society must move to a circular economy where everything is reused, renewed, or returned to the environment.

Be agnostic about growth

One chart in modern economics is so dangerous and problematic that it is never drawn or shown to its logical conclusion (see figure 5.4). This would be a chart showing unchecked and unconstrained economic growth. No system in nature can grow forever, but it is somehow assumed (and remains an almost unquestioned assumption among most economists) that unlimited economic growth is not only possible but desirable as well.

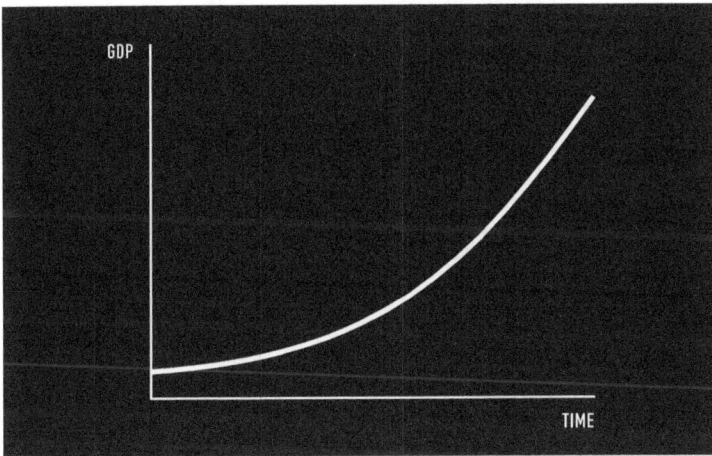

Figure 5.4. Unlimited—and unrealistic—growth.

In many ways, Raworth is the personification of Generation Re. She began by reimaging economics as a discipline that could meet the serious shortfall in human needs without overshooting the planetary constraints. She did so by reexamining existing economic dogma and challenging the assumption that unlimited economic growth is an unmitigated good. As Raworth and others have pointed out, unlimited growth is the ideology of a cancer cell; nothing in nature grows without limit without doing irreparable damage all around it.

Raworth also identified a gaping blind spot in most economists' thinking by pointing out the obvious: The modern economy is wholly embedded within the environment and not a separate, standalone entity. In this way, Raworth was seeing what others were not seeing—or were choosing not to see. By challenging conventional wisdom and working to redesign the field of economics, Raworth is also providing society an opportunity to change its view of who we are, where we stand, and what we aspire to become.

THE DOUGHNUT IN PRACTICE

"The day is not far off when the economic problem will take the back seat where it belongs, and the arena of the heart and head will be occupied and reoccupied by our real problems—the problems of life and human relations, of creation and behavior and religion."

—JOHN MAYNARD KEYNES

In 2025, the city of Amsterdam will celebrate its 750th anniversary. In a bold experiment that could lay the foundation for the next 750 years, the city is embracing doughnut economics. Amsterdam began the process by creating a city portrait, showing where the city is currently falling short in meeting the most basic needs of its citizens, along with where it is overshooting its planetary boundaries. Amsterdam's long-term vision is for all of the city's inhabitants to thrive within the ecological constraints of the planet.

As it stands today, Amsterdam's portrait is far from perfect. Twenty percent of its citizens are not able to meet their basic needs,[5] and the city is exceeding its limits on carbon dioxide emissions, fertilizer use, land use, and freshwater usage.

But Amsterdam has initiated Raworth's process by engaging in big-picture thinking. It is striving to view all of its actions through four different lenses—social, ecological, local, and global.

This planning has led city officials and citizens to begin taking action. The reality that a number of the city's residents cannot meet their daily dietary needs while, at the same time, the average resident of Amsterdam is wasting an average of 100 pounds of food a year led the city to get serious about using mobile food banks to redistribute excess food. The strategy is now combating hunger while simultaneously working to mitigate global ecological issues, including how unused food contributes to excessive land and fertilizer use.

The city has also begun to use the four lenses to ask a new set of questions: What does it mean to combine social goals with ecological goals, and how does it balance local aspirations with global responsibilities? These questions, in turn, are leading to actionable insights. Amsterdam knows, for instance, that it must continue to produce and manufacture new homes to combat a shortage of affordable housing, but this construction must be done in a manner that doesn't stress the natural environment. To better balance these competing needs, city officials now require more renewable energy be installed and a higher level of recycled materials to be used in the construction of all buildings. The combination has created housing not only that is more affordable to buy and operate but that also emits fewer greenhouse gases. The city is even encouraging builders to make more bird-friendly retaining walls and to use bee-hotel bricks. These steps are a way to create a more pollinator-friendly environment and better protect and enhance biodiversity.

In terms of tying local aspirations to global responsibilities, Amsterdam has taken a series of innovative steps, including encouraging the use of shared automobiles, which it hopes will reduce transportation costs for citizens while also creating more green space through the elimination of a number of parking spaces. In time, it is expected the spaces will be converted to tree-lined parks that will help clean the air, reduce the heat island effect, lower air-conditioning costs for residents, and eventually even help combat loneliness by becoming community gathering spots for neighborhood festivals.

Amsterdam's goal is to have a completely circular economy by 2050, and although it is far short of this goal today, its actions are serving to move the city's portrait into something closer to a real-time selfie that helps the city and its inhabitants better understand where progress is still needed.

By sharing its success stories, Amsterdam hopes to demonstrate how the city's transformation is already underway, but it also seeks to create the momentum to drive further change. To date, Portland and Philadelphia have also adopted portions of the doughnut approach. Amsterdam is actively working to create a city that can be assured of celebrating its 1500th anniversary in the year 2775.

REDESIGNING FOR VISIBILITY AND DIGNITY

Over 2 billion people are currently unbanked. These are individuals—including refugees, the displaced and homeless, and the world's poorest—whose economic contributions to the global supply chain are invisible. They have no credit history that would enable them to become bankable. Eradicating this invisibility is one of the most important elements in combating global poverty.

In 2015, Ashish Gadnis and Hamse Warfa started BanQu, the world's first digitally distributed economic identity platform. The company leverages blockchain technology and a user's mobile phone to create a digital electronic confirmation each time the user sells a product (often an agricultural crop) or delivers a product or service into the commercial marketplace. Digital solutions to these economic problems are viable because roughly 60 percent of those whom BanQu seeks to serve own mobile phones.[6]

This economic passport creates an accessible, secure digital record of every commercial transaction. It helps people document their participation in the global economy, providing the proof necessary to open a bank account, which was previously unavailable to them, despite decades of work, because paper receipts were not sufficient. Eventually, they can gain access to the financial capital necessary to grow their farms or small businesses, finance a child's education, or even start a cooperative with their neighbors. Tracked by BanQu's digital ledger, these essential workers not only become visible economic actors, but also their now-observable contributions create transparency up and down the supply chain that customers are increasingly seeking.

BanQu is now operating in over 40 countries and has provided digital identity and banking services to over 500,000 people. It is also working with Fortune 100 companies, including Coca-Cola, to ensure that everyone who participates in the global supply chain can become bankable.

REDESIGNING INVESTMENTS

*"The EDI is the single most interesting and
practical thing I've seen for fostering long-termism on
the part of both companies and investors."*

—ROBERT ECCLES, Harvard Business School

John Fullerton is a former managing director at J. P. Morgan who has come to believe the root cause of the ecological crisis is our economic system. Specifically, he believes that too many investors, without conscious awareness, are confusing speculation with investing and that their behavior has led to a series of unsustainable and unhealthy practices.

Instead of just complaining about the system, Fullerton decided to do something about it. He created Evergreen Direct Investing (EDI). Like Kate Raworth, Fullerton does not accept the assumption of unlimited growth and has, instead, come to believe that a far better model looks more like a healthy, consistently fruit-bearing apple tree. The long-term value of an apple tree does not come from its size but, rather, from its sustained ability to produce tasty, nutritious fruit over time. The same is true of businesses in Fullerton's investing model.

EDI seeks to do this by creating an investment structure that aligns the interests of institutional investors, such as pension funds, endowments, and universities, who are seeking consistent, long-term returns with the long-term interests of CEOs, leaders, and entrepreneurs, who have grown fatigued by the tyranny of short-term value maximization that Wall Street demands. Harmonization between business leaders and investors creates a win-win situation in which CEOs are free to focus on the longer-term interests of their companies, communities, and the planet, and investors get a fair return.

Fullerton's idea of regenerative investing works like this: The investors receive priority access to the cash flows from those businesses they invest in—in the form of a negotiated rate of return (say six or eight percent)—up until the point they receive their initial investment back. After that time, the investors still receive a fair but lower rate of return. This lower rate frees up money that allows management to both reward its employees and reinvest in the company.

This dynamic, which is also referred to as *slow money*, creates a triple-win situation. The investors get their money and a steady flow of income over the long term. The employees and management are motivated to keep the business sustainable over the long term, because they will receive a higher percentage of the profits after the initial investment has been paid off. And the environment is not overly exploited in the relentless pursuit of unlimited growth.

Fullerton's vision is revolutionary and potentially a paradigm shift, because it seeks to move investors' role away from short-term profit maximization to something more akin to an intergenerational trustee of capital.

REDESIGNING WITH VALUES

"Work is about a search for daily meaning as well as daily bread, for recognition as well as cash, for astonishment rather than torpor; in short, for a sort of life rather than a Monday through Friday sort of dying."

—STUDS TERKEL

Unilever

In 2010, Unilever unveiled the Unilever Sustainable Living Plan (USLP) and announced the company's intention to grow its business while also dramatically reducing its impact on the environment. At the time, many environmentalists were skeptical that the company, which manufactures over 400 brands and serves 2.5 billion customers, would make a meaningful change.

A decade later, the skeptics were silenced as Unilever reduced its waste footprint per consumer by 32 percent, achieved zero waste across all of its factories, reached 100 percent renewable grid electricity,[7] and merged the positions of chief marketing officer (CMO) and head of sustainability into a single position. In an interconnected world, it realized it couldn't simultaneously have one person focused on selling products while another worked to reduce the company's environmental impact.

Unilever is far from perfect, and its leaders are refreshingly candid in admitting where it has fallen short of its own environmental aspirations in key areas, such as reducing first-use plastic and ridding its supply chain of deforestation. But these shortcomings have only served to fuel the ambitions of the company's successor plan to the USLP—Unilever Compass. The new initiative is centered on three core beliefs: Brands with purpose grow, companies with purpose last, and people with purpose thrive. It is a serious attempt to redesign around a commitment to purpose.

The reunion of head and heart is essential not only for individuals but for large corporations as well, and Unilever is showing a path forward. Its Compass initiative is a serious attempt to reconnect its business with the heart of its founder, William Lever, who believed that business required a solid spiritual foundation if it were to prosper over the long term. This belief prompted Lever to take a series of actions that may not sound bold today but that were revolutionary at the end of the nineteenth century. Among other things, Lever instituted an eight-hour workday, created a pension system, and established health and unemployment benefits for all of his employees. Lever also paid his workers a fair wage, held self-improvement courses in arts and music, and created a community of affordable housing for his employees and their families.

Skeptics may be forgiven if they think the focus on purpose is little more than corporate pabulum, but Unilever's actions suggest otherwise. As part of Unilever Compass, the company announced its intention to become a net-zero carbon company (meaning it takes as much carbon out of the environment as it contributes) by 2039. This is meaningful because the goal is 11 years sooner than required by the Paris Agreement on climate change, demonstrating a genuine commitment rather than merely meeting externally imposed goals.

Unilever is also[8]

- Investing $1.5 billion in a new climate fund that will focus heavily on reforesting

- Cutting its use of first-use plastics and planning on making all plastic reusable, recyclable, or compostable by 2025

- Favoring suppliers that have set science-based targets for carbon reduction

- Actively lobbying governments around the world for ambitious environmental policies, such as carbon pricing

- Removing petrochemicals from many of its products

- Using cloud computing, satellite imagery, and artificial intelligence to bring heightened transparency to its supply chain

- Creating nano factories to manufacture small batches of its products as close to its customers as possible (and lower CO_2 emissions)

- And paying dairy farmers to invest in regenerative agriculture techniques

There are three practical takeaways from Unilever's efforts.

Doing the right thing for the planet also benefits the bottom line

Since 2010, Unilever has avoided over $2 billion in costs by embracing innovative packaging solutions and slashing costs through improvements in water and energy usage.[9]

Sustainability is a growth business

Unilever's Sustainable Living Brands (Dove, Lifebuoy, Ben & Jerry's, and Comfort) have grown twice as fast as the rest of its portfolio. This suggests that customers will support brands that are striving to do the right thing for the planet.

The company's focus on purpose is resonating with prospective employees

After Google and Apple, Unilever is the third most searched for company on LinkedIn. This is impressive, because Unilever, as a manufacturer of household products, may lack the cachet of tech companies. In 2021, over 2 million people applied for positions at the company,[10] ensuring that Unilever is able to continue to attract talented and motivated employees.

There is one final insight that businesses can take away from Unilever's commitment to sustainability and purpose. The company is doubling down on these areas of focus because it understands this simple but often overlooked truth: The modern economy is embedded in—and wholly dependent on—the natural environment. If there is no healthy planet, there is no future for Unilever or any other business.

Best Buy

In 2012, Best Buy was left for dead by most people, and there wasn't a single Wall Street analyst who rated its stock (then $11 a share) as a buy. Amazon, the giant online retailer, was dominating the e-commerce space, and other leading technology companies, including Apple, Microsoft, and Sony, were opening physical stores to compete directly with Best Buy.

Into this dire situation stepped Hubert Joly. As an effective and practical executive, he immediately set about fixing what was broken. Best Buy enhanced its online presence, became price competitive with other retailers, and turned its stores from an expensive liability into a strategic asset by using them as distribution centers to quickly ship products to its customers. These actions helped neutralize their competitor's strategic advantages.

Once the ship was righted, Joly focused on people. His first action was to shift Best Buy's purpose from being a leading consumer electronics company to embracing what Joly called "a noble purpose"—in this case, "enriching lives through technology by addressing key human needs."[11] The centerpiece of this new purpose was Renew Blue, a broad initiative focused on helping customers demystify technology and assisting people in finding the best product, service, or solution to meet their unique needs.

Equally important, Joly turned his attention to his employees' personal goals and sought to connect them to the company's new purpose. He did this by taking a series of uncommon actions and asking some un-corporation-like questions. For example, Joly asked employees to bring in pictures of themselves when they were three or four years old; then, he asked them what their dreams were at that time. In other meetings, he asked his team to reflect on how they want to be remembered in life and even encouraged them to write their retirement speeches as a way to anchor their personal aspirations to the company's work.

Over his eight-year tenure, Joly increased Best Buy's share price from $11 to over $110—a 1,000 percent increase—and he did it by openly leading with heart and soul.[12] He also espouses a unique, un-corporate philosophy, which he expresses with the phrase "I am seen; therefore, I am."

Joly understood it was his job to see his employees and help them find meaning and fulfillment in their work. In doing so, he created an environment where human magic could be unleashed. It was this human magic, Joly believes, that allowed Best Buy to thrive and grow.

These are inspiring aims and remarkable results, but naturally, there is always more work to be done within the aspirations of Generation Re. As CEO, Joly made 475 times the average frontline Best Buy employee's wages, and it could be argued that he could have done a better job sharing the company's profits with both shareholders and employees. Nevertheless, he did save 125,000 jobs and demonstrated that it is possible to follow a noble purpose and successfully run a profitable business by focusing on people first.

REDESIGNING FOR WORK—LIFE BALANCE

In the spring of 2018, Perpetual Guardian, a 240-employee New Zealand company that manages wills, estates, and trusts conducted a two-month experiment and shifted all of its employees to a four-day workweek with no cut in pay. The experiment was so successful that the company agreed to adopt the policy permanently by the year's end.

Perpetual Guardian's key finding was that overall productivity increased by 20 percent. The finding, which was verified by an independent third-party audit, suggested that productivity increased because the staff became more creative, the number of meetings was reduced, and work attendance improved. Other positive benefits included the employees reporting a 24 percent increase in work—life balance and a reduction in stress by 7 percent.[13]

A similar large-scale experiment was conducted in Iceland from 2015 to 2019. It involved 2,500 workers (almost one percent of the country's entire workforce) reducing the number of hours they worked from 40 to 36 without a reduction in pay or benefits. The results mirrored those found at Perpetual Guardian: The vast majority of the employees experienced greater happiness without a loss in productivity.

Since that time, Scotland, Spain, and Japan have unveiled plans to launch trials around the four-day workweek. In the summer of 2021, Aziz Hasan, the CEO of Kickstarter, announced his company's intention

continued

to adopt a 32-hour workweek in 2022 and said in a statement discussing his rationale for the policy change that he believes everyone who works for Kickstarter should have the ability to advance the company's goals forward while also spending more time with families and friends, pursuing their own creative and artistic projects, and engaging with the causes that are important to them.[14]

In a related development, a growing number of countries, including France, Italy, Spain, Chile, Ireland, Slovakia, and the Philippines, have also adopted right-to-disconnect laws, which provide workers the right not to respond to digital communications after hours.

REDESIGNING FOR COMMUNITY

For most of her professional career, Hilary Cottam has created alternative welfare systems in the United Kingdom and, more recently, in other parts of the world. Unlike some researchers and academics, Cottam has spent a great deal of time living among the people she seeks to assist. One of her significant insights is that, in the name of efficiency, many social welfare bureaucracies have designed human relationships out of the system. This doesn't sound like a groundbreaking insight, but as Cottam herself said, "I used to be the person with a radical idea. Now I'm the person with the idea that seems like common sense."[15]

Cottam's work in two areas—unemployment and elderly care—has produced impressive results, and both have benefitted from putting human relationships and connections back at the center of the system.

With the unemployed, she begins by first asking them not how long they have been out of work or what their qualifications are but, rather, by asking, "What do you dream of being, and who is the first person you need to know to connect you to that dream?"[16]

Over time, in the handful of communities that have adopted Cottam's ideas, she has created a sort of mycelium network of people who can help the unemployed make connections. This is significant because a lack of accessibility to supportive networks is a key impediment to rebuilding a life after episodes of unemployment, particularly for the poor. Early results suggest that her system outperformed the existing system by a factor of three and at a fraction of the cost.[17]

Regarding the issue of elderly care, Cottam points out that loneliness is a bigger killer than smoking, but, in many industrialized countries, little is being done to alleviate it. (The United Kingdom is an exception; it has created the role of *minister for loneliness* to bring more public attention to the issue.) Cottam's solution is simple and elegant: Nurture human bonds. This includes allowing people to select their own social workers and then allowing these workers to get to know their clients on a personal basis by inviting them out of their homes to engage in ordinary activities such as going to the park, the movies, or the theater.

In some ways, Cottam is reinventing old ideas in new ways. At the turn of the century in America, before the welfare system had become institutionalized, it was not uncommon to find mutual-aid societies that catered to specific groups of people that were often based on ethnicity but that served as human networks that new arrivals and others in need could tap into for assistance.

The challenge, as is often the case with significant shifts in thinking, is not in getting people to see where the existing system is not working. It is in inspiring and motivating others, including those in positions of power, to see the new wisdom that is being revealed and then, if necessary, persuading them to cede power so that these new ideas can flourish.

REDESIGNING POLITICS

In the United States, Jeanne Massey is not well known even in her home state, but she is the persistent voice of FairVote Minnesota, a nonprofit, nonpartisan organization pursuing a procedural voting reform that could have revolutionary implications for democracy not only in Minnesota but throughout the United States as well. The system is known as ranked-choice voting, and it allows voters to rank candidates by preference rather than choosing a single candidate. The strength of the system lies when three or more candidates are in a race.

Under most local, state, and federal voting systems in the United States, the winner is determined by plurality: Whichever candidate receives the most votes wins, regardless of whether they receive a majority of the vote. Consider a hypothetical case where three candidates from across the political spectrum run for office. After the first vote, the candidate for party A receives 45.01 percent of the vote, the candidate for party B has 45.00 percent of the vote, and the candidate for party C receives 9.99 percent. Under the existing system, candidate A would, by virtue of receiving just .01 percent more of the votes than candidate B, be determined to be the winner, despite 54.99 percent of the voters having selected other candidates.

Ranked-choice voting asks a different question: What is the will of the majority of the voters? The process of ranking candidates allows this answer to emerge. By providing voters with the opportunity to rank their candidates according to their preference, it can be determined which candidate was the second choice of the voters who voted for Party C's candidate. (Candidate C, because they came in last, is eliminated from the race but their second choice is tallied on behalf of that candidate.)

Ranked-choice voting does not favor one political party over another. It simply allows the will of the majority to be captured in multiple-candidate races. This system also has a multitude of benefits. First, it strengthens the community by ensuring the majority of its constituents are represented according to their will. Next, by eliminating the spoiler effect (when a person's vote, usually for a third-party candidate, has the unintended consequence of helping the candidate they most detest), it allows people to vote for the candidate who most closely aligns with their values and positions, rather than having to engage in strategic voting.

For example, in the current system, a conservative voter who leans libertarian may not vote for the Libertarian Party's candidate because they worry that conservative votes will be spread across the Libertarian and Republican candidates. In a ranked-voting system, this voter could vote for their preferred candidate, knowing that, if they don't receive a majority of votes, the vote won't harm the Republican, who may share their belief on a more limited role for government. On the liberal side, a supporter of, say, a Green Party candidate could vote for that candidate knowing that if the candidate doesn't win a majority, they won't hurt a more progressive candidate who shares some but not all of their beliefs.

In this way, ranked-choice voting allows more voices to be represented in elections. It also has the added benefit of bringing new issues into the political realm, regardless of their current popularity. For instance, in the near future, it is plausible that a political party may form that advocates for universal basic income, legal rights for natural resources or animals, the decriminalization of psilocybin (hallucinogenic mushrooms), or some other "fringe" political issue. While it is possible that the candidates from such single-issue parties could win a majority of votes in some races, it is unlikely under the present winner-take-all system. This third party, however, if it begins to receive more support from the community could send a powerful signal to the more mainstream political parties to consider adding the issue to its platform. In this way, new issues may move into the political discourse sooner than might otherwise happen. To return to the metaphor of a murmuration, ranked-choice voting brings voters into the system while simultaneously shifting the direction of the entire flock.

Another benefit of ranked-choice voting is that it changes the dynamics of politics. Over the past few decades, few people would disagree that the political climate in the United States (and many other areas of the world) has become increasingly polarized. What is unique about the ranked-choice approach is that, in an effort to be ranked as the second choice of voters, candidates are incentivized to emphasize those areas where they agree with their opponents. In this way, ranked-choice voting opens the door for communication and compromise because it highlights areas where candidates share similar positions. As an added benefit, it might also reduce the number of negative attack ads that blanket the airwaves during election season.

Since Massey has been the executive director of FairVote Minnesota, she has proven instrumental in having ranked-choice voting adopted in Minnesota's three largest cities. Her expertise has also been critical in helping ranked-choice voting gain traction in Maine, which, in 2018, became the first state to adopt it for statewide races, including governor, US Senate, and Congress. Starting in 2021, New York City began using ranked-choice voting in primaries and special elections.

REDESIGNING FOR BEAUTY

"For he who would proceed aright . . . should begin in youth to visit beautiful forms . . . out of that he should create fair thoughts; and soon he will of himself perceive that the beauty of one form is akin to the beauty of another, and that beauty in every form is one and the same," said Plato.[18]

What if we could walk through the world every day immersed in art and beauty—not because we ourselves are artists (although everyone is at some level) but because humans have decided to reexamine public spaces through the lens of what uplifts the human spirit, inspires the human heart, and opens the mind to greater possibility? Consider how ordinary public elements such as light posts, crosswalks, bridges, hallways, and even directional signage could be imbued with artistry and spirit-raising intrigue.

As we come to understand that there is no reason human creativity cannot be integrated into such everyday things (overcoming assumptions about how it's "always been done"), such redesign could become an established norm. And if we were to encounter these beguiling and colorful surroundings, perhaps they would momentarily awaken us from sleepwalking-type habits that can dull our days and instead foster moments of everyday joy—maybe even bring to life something important that has lain dormant within us. What if, in our social and environmental crisis and unrest, the human need for beauty were to be seen as a vital force, an elemental yearning that, if attended to, would make transformational change more possible and more effective?

continued

Figure 5.5. During the financial crisis of 2008, the city of Akureyi, Iceland installed red heart stop lights to boost citizens' spirits, beautify the city, and remind peopole of what mattered most.

REDESIGNING FOR TIME

Can something be forever new and forever ancient? If the question sounds like a koan, it is not. Since 690 BCE, the Ise Jingu Shrine, in Japan, has been torn down and rebuilt to the same approximate design every 20 years to reflect the Shinto belief of the death and renewal of nature, to represent the impermanence of all things, and as a practical way to transfer building skills from one generation to the next.

Another interesting development coming out of Japan is the Future Design movement, inspired by the Native American principle of seven generation thinking that seeks to ensure that every decision works for future descendants. The movement is a unique type of citizens' assembly in which one group of participants takes the position of current residents and another group imagines themselves to be residents in the year 2060, two generations out. The latter are even provided ceremonial robes to enhance their imaginations and to remind them of their special obligation to those future generations.

To date, the movement has conducted assemblies in dozens of municipalities across Japan and has consistently developed more progressive plans than the ones developed by elected officials, who are often motivated by short-term political considerations. The assemblies, however, offer the politicians some cover for adopting these less conventional—sometimes even radical—proposals.

The Future Design assemblies may seem unusual, but democracy has taken a great many forms since it was first invented 2,500 years ago, and it is likely to keep being redesigned. Even Thomas Jefferson, one of America's most prominent founders, believed that "the tree of liberty must be refreshed from time to time." He once even remarked, "God forbid we should ever be 20 years without such a rebellion."

REDESIGNING FOR A LONGER-TERM PERSPECTIVE

The Long-Term Stock Exchange (LTSE) was founded in 2021 to provide a market-based signal for companies and investors who share a long-term commitment to sustainable practices and would like to place a greater emphasis on environmental, social, and governance issues. The stock exchange was conceived by Eric Reis to encourage long-term thinking over short-term quarterly earnings.

Companies that list shares for sale on the LTSE will be required to publish a series of policies that focus on long-term value creation. The exchange's key principles hold that long-term focused companies should consider a broader group of stakeholders, including employees, the community, and the natural environment; that these companies should measure success in years and decades, not quarters; and that executive and board compensation must be aligned with the long-term focus.

continued

At the current time, only two companies, Twilio and Asana (both multibillion-dollar software companies) are presently listed on the LTSE. As more executives, boards of directors, and investors seek ways to better cultivate enduring value in the public marketplace, the list of companies wishing to be listed on the exchange could grow. It is a trend worth monitoring.

A WORLD WIRED FOR INTERCONNECTION

The word *interconnection* may seem touchy-feely to many people, especially those in the business world. But humans are uniquely considered among animals to cooperate in large numbers to advance projects for the common good.[19]

Margaret Mead, the famous anthropologist, was once asked what the first sign of human civilization was. To the surprise of many, Mead did not mention the invention of language or the written word, nor did she speak about the development of agriculture or the creation of cities, states, or governments. Mead said the first sign of civilization was a healed broken bone—a femur. For her, the act was a clear and compelling sign that a human being had cared enough for a fellow human being to nurse that individual back to health. In this sense, Mead believed civilization was born of our innate need for human connection. It is impossible to know what that first healer was thinking, but clearly, something other than a short-term, selfish interest was at play for the care provider to take the time and energy to nurse the other person back to health.

Humans, nature, and the universe also appear interconnected by design. The neurons in the brain, the vessels pumping blood from the heart; the mycelium networks in the ground; the veins in a leaf; the branches in a tree; the network of brooks, streams, and rivers that flow to the sea; and even the clusters of galaxies in the universe form intricate networks that bespeak interconnection. Is it too much to believe that the long-term success of business rests on a similar process of nurturing a flow between humans, communities, nature, and life, and that the existing paradigm of the individual separate self is dying?

SKILLS AND INSIGHTS FOR REDESIGNING

Following are a set of practices, skills, and insights that can help foster the sense of interconnectedness that is key to the ethos of Generation Re and to redesigning a regenerative future.

Practice relationality

"You must do everything with the awareness that everything, in some way, connects to everything else."

—LEONARDO DA VINCI

When you see another person from across the room or gaze upon a farm field, the idea that all is interconnected may seem neither real nor evident. To begin to see these invisible interconnections, consider the simple act of buying a mango at your local grocery store. Before you could eat the mango, a clerk had to ring it up. Someone had to stock it. Another worker had to load it off the truck. A truck driver had to transport it. A farm laborer had to pick it. And a farmer needed to grow it.

Dig a little deeper, and you'll see the connections don't stop there. Someone had to build the farm equipment that harvested the mango, the truck that shipped it, and the grocery store that sold it. At a deeper level still, the land that the farmer grew the mango on had to be sustainably maintained for generations. The mango tree itself was also dependent on a rich ecosystem of insects, animals, forests, and rivers for its growth. Even the oceans are involved, helping create the weather that allows the mango to grow. Even further in time, the water that helped grow the mango is approximately 3 billion years old, and the atoms of the mango are estimated to be 10 billion years old, forged in the heart of a star.

If a simple mango can connect a person to countless people, things, and matter across time and space, it is not hard to fathom why Leonardo da Vinci said, "You must do everything with the awareness that everything, in some way, connects to everything else."

A modest example of two large corporations trying to practice relationality as it pertains to the plant and animal world and our larger ecosystem are General Mills and Cargill. Both companies are now actively engaged in regenerative agriculture, which works with nature to pull carbon from the air and store it in the soil. It also uses fewer pesticides and synthetic fertilizers, while also serving to enrich the soil by creating a healthy ecosystem for microorganisms, worms, insects, and animals. General Mills has 70,000 acres currently enrolled in regenerative agriculture practices and intends to scale up to 1 million acres by 2030.[20] Cargill plans on employing regenerative agriculture across 10 million acres of North American farmland in the next decade in an effort to mitigate the effects of climate change, regenerate soil, and improve water use.[21]

A bolder example of a community practicing relationality is Curridabat, Costa Rica. Known as the "Sweet City," Curridabat granted citizenship to bees, bats, hummingbirds, butterflies, trees, and native plants in 2019, because it understood the role pollinators and pollinator-friendly plants and crops play in creating a healthy and vibrant ecosystem.

The federal government of New Zealand has taken a similar step by granting legal personhood to the Whanganui River in response to a century-long petition by the Maori people (the indigenous people of New Zealand); for them, the river was—and is—a living relation.

The notion was beautifully captured by a Native American elder who, when speaking to a group of business students at a leading university, said, "What you call *natural resources*, we call relatives." That's relationality. Thankfully, the notion of viewing and perceiving nature as a living relation is slowly gathering momentum in Western society.

Redesign with people in mind

*"You think because you understand 'one' you must
also understand 'two,' because one and one make two.
But you must also understand 'and.'"*

—RUMI

There is a well-known story of an anthropologist who lived among a remote African tribe. One day, he filled a basket with a rich assortment of delicious fruits and placed it near a tree. He then organized a foot race among the children and told them that whoever reached the basket first would win the entire basket of fruit.

When the anthropologist told the children to run, he was shocked when they all clasped hands and ran as one to the basket, where they then sat under the tree and enjoyed their bounty together. When the anthropologist asked one of the children why the fastest child did not just run to the basket and claim the prize for themselves, the child responded, "How can one of us be happy if all the others are sad?" This philosophical outlook is beautifully captured in the African word *ubuntu*, which means "I am because we are." It is the belief in a universal bond that connects all humanity.

The story is a powerful example of horizontal relationality. In contrast to vertical relating, which places people within a hierarchy premised on unequal power structures, horizontal relating places all people on an equal plane, allowing a sense that we are all walking alongside one another as fellow travelers in life.

Alex Stephany discovered the magic of horizontal relating as the founder and CEO of BEAM, the world's first platform to crowdsource training for homeless people and support them as they find work related to their skills and training. Stephany started BEAM after befriending a homeless man in London and realizing how ineffective his good deeds of providing food and clothing were in addressing the root cause of the man's situation. Stephany talked at length with his homeless companion to find out what the man truly needed.

Stephany discovered that retraining is often prohibitively expensive for those living on the street. For others, he learned the main barrier was transportation or childcare. As a technologist, Stephany resolved to create a world-class platform that understood the unique needs and desires of its customers but then matched them with people willing to assist them financially and stay with them until they receive sufficient training to gain full-time employment and secure private housing. To date, BEAM has helped hundreds of individuals in the greater London area,[22] and Stephany has plans to scale the program throughout the United Kingdom and around the world.

Redesign with the future in mind

"The most important question we must ask ourselves is, Are we being good ancestors?"

—JONAS SALK

Clocks didn't have minute hands until the 1700s and didn't have second hands until the 1800s. Soon after the development of the modern clock, railways, mass production, and assembly lines were all created, and each focused even more attention on time. This trend continues today in everything from e-commerce to the stock market, where time is now measured in milliseconds and even nanoseconds. Given this seemingly relentless focus on ever smaller increments of time, is it any wonder that individuals, organizations, and civilizations alike have difficulty thinking and acting with a long-term perspective?

Nevertheless, if humanity is to survive, it is time to use new—or, rather, old—conceptions about time as one basis for redesigning our future. In his 2020 book, *The Good Ancestor*, Roman Krznaric shares a picture of a massive slice of a giant sequoia in the American Museum of Natural History in New

York City. The tree's 1,342 rings reveal that it dates back to the middle of the sixth century, and the discerning observer can identify specific rings that correspond to historical events that occurred over the tree's lengthy life. This idea is known as *tree time*, and author Richard Power recommends experiencing life "at the speed of wood." It serves as another component of redesigning for a thriving world.

Figure 5.6.

There is an apocryphal story about the New College at Oxford University (which, in spite of its name, was actually built over 600 years ago, in 1379). In 1860, it was discovered that the large oak beams supporting the college's ceiling had been infested by beetles and were in need of being replaced. At the time, finding beams of a comparable size and girth was deemed impossible since most of England's large oak trees had long since been felled and harvested. Not knowing what to do, someone suggested looking for suitable oaks on the college's outer lands, which were scattered about the country. When they consulted the college's forester, they were stunned to discover that not only did he have oaks of the suitable size, but he had also been waiting for someone to contact him. They learned he, as well as the long lineage of the college's foresters before him, had been maintaining a special grove of oaks that had been planted at the time of the college's construction for the sole purpose of replacing the beams when they became "beetled." Whether the story is true or not, it conveys a larger truth: To survive into the future, we must think at the speed of wood.

As a recent example, consider Notre Dame Cathedral, which almost burned to the ground in a horrific fire in the spring of 2019. Two years later, desperate to rebuild the cathedral's iconic wooden spire, the French government scoured the French countryside in search of oak trees large enough to be used to rebuild the massive spire. How much better would it have been if, back in 1859, when the spire was originally added to the cathedral, farsighted leaders at Notre Dame had planned for that possibility and actually planted an oak grove?

Playing off the theme of cathedrals, a compelling way of thinking about thinking at the speed of wood is captured in the term *cathedral thinking*. The basic concept of cathedral thinking is to embrace a vision so big that it can't be completed in a single person's lifetime. Consider the Basílica de la Sagrada Família in Barcelona. Designed in 1882 by Antoni Gaudi, the cathedral is not expected to be completed until 2026; it has so far involved the labor of six successive generations.

Cathedral thinking need not be limited only to real cathedrals. A handful of business leaders, including the former CEO of

Duke Energy, Jim Rogers, have used the concept to reposition how employees think about their work. In Rogers's case, he used cathedral thinking to explain Duke Energy's transition away from coal and toward renewable energy. Rogers explained that the transition would not only position the company for long-term success, but it would also tether today's employees to future generations, who would benefit from the transition to cleaner and more sustainable forms of energy. Time will tell whether Rogers's vision of cathedral thinking will bake itself into the culture of Duke Energy, but if business leaders can elevate the aspirations of their business beyond the singular focus of short-term profits, they can provide a powerful mechanism for their employees to find meaning in their work by connecting them to future generations.

The list of social, environmental, and political challenges confronting society is well documented: climate change, poverty, homelessness, racial injustice, inequality, pollution, a lack of energy, restoring clean water, the loss of biodiversity, and the list goes on. It is unlikely that these issues will be solved in a single lifetime, but, rather than scaring away businesses, this reality should draw you into a world of exciting possibilities. One of the most powerful aspects of cathedral thinking is that it is not necessary to know how to solve the entire problem before you start implementing steps to a solution in your business. In the case of real cathedrals, the designers often did not know how the vaulted ceilings would be constructed, but they trusted that future generations, given enough time, would solve the problem.

Redesign for interconnection

"Here's where redesign begins in earnest, where we stop trying
to be less bad and we start figuring out how to be good."

—WILLIAM MCDONOUGH

The concept of a sharing economy is not new. Since 1979, the city of Berkeley has had a tool-lending library that allows people with home improvement projects to check out over 3,500 different tools, including saws, hammers, grouters, and even gardening tools.

Recall how Brooklyn Microgrid is leveraging blockchain technology to allow community-based producers of renewable energy to sell the excess energy they generate to their neighbors. This is, itself, an exciting and disruptive development, but it is just the proverbial tip of the iceberg of how businesses can leverage blockchain to foster an even deeper connection with their community.

Blockchain may also be a vehicle for sharing so much more. For example, it has been estimated that the average drill is used for only 13 minutes in its entire lifetime.[23] For most drill owners, the device sits idle except for that brief time it's performing its purpose, proving the old adage that most people don't want a drill; they want a hole.

By better tracking where the drill is, how long it is used, and the condition in which it was returned, blockchain can facilitate sharing a single drill more widely across a community. A business model for drills will still exist, but it will be based on a model that allows community members to pay only for that small fraction of the time they actually use the drill.

This concept may also be extended to automobiles (the average car sits idle 22 hours a day[24]), lawnmowers, snow blowers, ladders, boats, and even certain types of accessories, such as coats, purses, and jewelry. Not only will community members save money, but also the impact on the environment will be significantly lessened, because fewer objects—many of which have a sizable carbon footprint—will not need to be manufactured.

More innovative still are ideas about sharing time and the ownership of capital. The Swiss city of St. Gallen has created an innovative system called *Zeitvorsorge*, which translates into "time provisions." The system allows citizens 60 years or older to earn care-time credits by helping elderly citizens with a range of daily activities, including shopping, cooking, and cleaning. In addition to helping people bank credits for that future time when they will need similar care, it benefits the current residents by helping them maintain their independence longer and combat loneliness.

COOPERATION JACKSON

Started in 2013 in Jackson, Mississippi, and inspired by the Mondragon Cooperative in Spain (which consists of 257 cooperatives and almost 75,000 members[25]), Cooperation Jackson's goal is to create an entirely new supportive economy in which the residents of Jackson can live, work, grow, and thrive in a truly regenerative system.

Cooperation Jackson started from a basic premise: The existing economic and political system wasn't working for a majority of the city's Black residents. The medium income of Black residents in Jackson was $33,000 in 2017, and over one-third are living in poverty.[26] The cooperative's aim is to build an alternative system that helps workers take ownership of their work, and it has created a small but growing network of cooperatives and worker-owned enterprises, including Freedom Farms (an urban farming cooperative), a cafe and catering business, and a landscaping business.

The vision is to create a sustainable, regenerative system where the farm cooperative serves the cafe and catering business and the compost from those businesses is picked up by the landscaping business and returned to the farm cooperative. Cooperation Jackson is also working to develop a production cooperative, complete with a digital fabricator and 3D printer, to begin creating a village of sustainable housing for low-income residents.

The long-term goal is to create a federation of local worker cooperatives, a co-op incubator, a co-op education and training center, and a co-op bank to create a regenerative economic and political system that exists alongside today's capitalist system.

NEW VOCABULARY FOR NEW THINKING

New words, or new vocabularies, are often required to support new ways of thinking and perceiving. We invite you to consider the following. The linguist Jules Davidoff discovered that the Himba tribe in Namibia has a rich assortment of different words for the color green but no word for the color blue.[27] In an experiment, Davidoff placed 11 identical green squares in a circle and added one with a slightly different hue of green (figure 5.7). Most of the members of the Himba tribe could immediately spot the difference. He showed the same diagram to a group of English speakers, and the vast majority were unable to distinguish the square that was a different shade of green. If you have problems discerning the difference in color in the green square that is circled in yellow, don't worry. It may only be because you don't have a word for that particular hue of green.

Distinguishable by
Himba tribe

Figure 5.7. Davidoff's circle of greens. (URL in credits)

In a separate experiment, Davidoff then placed 11 identical green squares with one blue square, and the results were reversed. English speakers could readily identify the blue square, whereas the Himba could not easily distinguish the blue square (figure 5.8).

Distinguishable by
English speakers

Figure 5.8. Davidoff's blue. (URL in credits)

John Koenig is the author of *The Dictionary of Obscure Sorrows* and makes new words for ideas that don't currently have one in the English dictionary. One of these is *sonder*, a noun that he beautifully and lyrically defines as "the realization that each random passerby is living a life as vivid and complex as your own—populated with their own ambitions, friends, routines, worries, and inherited craziness—an epic story that continues invisibly around you like an anthill sprawling deep underground, with elaborate passageways to thousands of other lives that you'll never know existed, in which you might appear only once, as an extra sipping coffee in the background, as a blur of traffic passing on the highway, as a lighted window at dusk."[28]

Davidoff's experiment is a vivid example of how language influences how people see the world. Our personal experience of reality is not as objective as we believe it to be. Moreover, because our culture is shaped by language, it must be understood that it is just a lens through which we view the world. And it is prone, like other cultural lenses, to have distortions.

By way of analogy, consider the following optical illusion. It appears as though the circles are different colors—green, orange, and blue. Remarkably, though, the circles are the exact same color (see figures 5.9 and 5.10). We see the circles as distinct colors because the lines going through them are different colors. In this same way, think of languages (yours or others) as a filter that creates the experience of individual and unique realities. This does not mean that one perceived reality is right and the other is wrong. It is simply to underscore the importance of understanding that how we see the world is subjective (though we so often fall into believing our thoughts are objective truth).

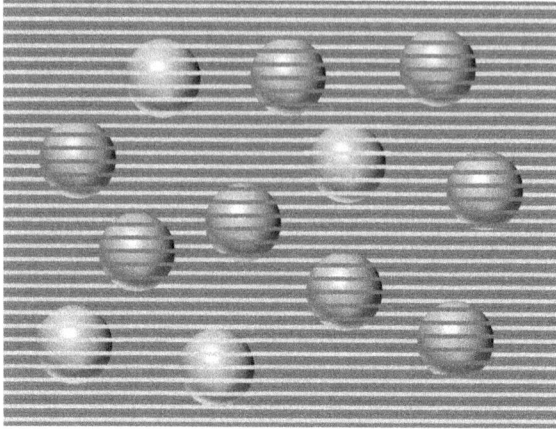

Figure 5.9. Color relativity. (URL in credits)

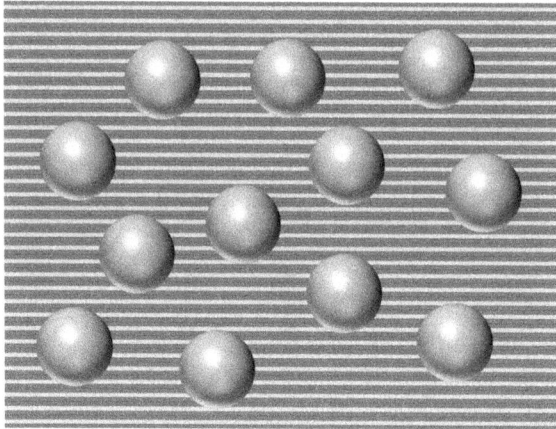

Figure 5.10. True color revealed. (URL in credits)

This fluidity in perception also suggests that a new vocabulary is needed to support the advancing ethos of Generation Re. Imagine our current language as a shaded filter that only allows us to see the world and its inhabitants as separate objects. Now imagine the shade was removed from that filter, allowing concepts into our consciousness that bespeak a unity, a similarity, an interconnectedness. New language can, indeed, open the mind to new realities.

The Japanese concept of kokoro, which combines mind, body, and spirit, allows concepts that the English language has separated into distinct categories to be reunited. This word, if its meaning were actively embraced, could enable us—particularly those in leadership positions who are pressured to think otherwise—to accept matters of the heart and spirit as legitimate concerns. It may not be long before the English language possesses such a word.

The Zulu greeting *sawubona* literally means "I see you,"[29] and carries the recognition that "you are important to me, and I value you."[30] The term conveys the relationality of people and the importance of each person's inherent sacred value. Sawubona reminds leaders of the importance of not simply viewing employees in terms of the roles they perform but as whole individuals who embody skills and talents, with hopes, desires, fears, and sorrows.

The Lakota have a phrase, *mitákuye oyás'iŋ*, which translates to "we are all related" or "all my relations." The phrase acknowledges the sacredness of all things—humans, animals, plants, waters, rocks, and the cosmos. This essential phrase reflects how the Lakota see the natural environment not as a resource to be exploited but as relatives and, therefore, something to be respected and nurtured.

In a world where our dependence on one another, our local and global community, and the natural world is becoming more evident, redesigning for this new awareness is essential if we are to continue to thrive. Embracing concepts like kokoro, sawubona, and mitákuye oyás'iŋ (along with concepts not yet created) will help us build evolutionary designs based on the reality of our interconnectedness.

Chapter 6

RECONSIDER

"Reality is merely an illusion, albeit a very persistent one."

—ALBERT EINSTEIN

P lato's cave is arguably the most famous and influential allegory in the history of human thought. In it, the Greek philosopher constructs a dialogue between his brother, Glaucon, and his mentor, Socrates. At its heart, the allegory asks the question *Do you value* your *truth or* the *truth?*

Plato asks us to imagine a cave where people have been imprisoned since childhood and their legs and neck are shackled, such that they can't turn around. All they can see is the wall in front of them. Behind them is a fire, and in front of the fire (yet behind the prisoners) is a raised walkway where people can walk. These people cast shadows on the wall of the cave, and because this is all the prisoners can see, they come to accept the shadows as real objects and, therefore, their reality.

In time, one of the prisoners is freed, but, because he has spent his whole life in darkness, his eyes are blinded by the light of the fire. So painful is the experience that the prisoner seeks to return to his shackles—and all he has ever known. Instead, the prisoner is dragged past the fire, out of the cave, and into the blazing sunlight. This light is even brighter than the fire, and again, the prisoner begs to return to the cave. Slowly, the freed man's eyes adjust, and for the first time, he sees shapes and objects and then people, water, the stars, and the moon. Eventually, he can even look at the sun. Before, the prisoner was only seeing illusions he thought were real; now, he sees real objects.

Amazed at all he has seen, the former prisoner returns to the cave, eager to share his newly acquired wisdom. But, his eyes having now grown accustomed to the sunlight, he is blinded by the darkness of the cave. The other prisoners come to believe the journey harmed him and that, therefore, it would be dangerous and foolish for them to undertake a similar journey.

A major transformation is taking place today, and a new understanding of reality is emerging that will render some of our present operating assumptions mere illusions. The key task before us is to understand the ways our view of reality is limited and to open our hearts and minds to see the possibilities within an expanded perception of reality.

THE REALNESS OF THE INVISIBLE

Consider how new ways of seeing the world overturned old paradigms. The telescope was instrumental in helping Copernicus and Galileo come to new understandings of reality when they used it to verify that the earth was not at the center of the universe. The microscope also played a similar role in overturning previous conceptions as scientists came to better understand reality by seeing what was previously invisible to the human eye, including germs, atoms, quarks and, most recently, muons. (The latter is a super tiny particle that many physicists now believe will require science to rethink many long-held assumptions about how the universe operates).[1]

There is no doubt our existing sense of reality is incomplete, and so we invite you to reconsider: Could our understanding of reality extend far beyond what common perception suggests?

Using the microscope and telescope as the basis for our own (admittedly crude) allegory, imagine having both an incredibly powerful microscope and telescope. The former is so good that you can look at your hand which, of course, appears and feels real, but what you would discover under the lens of this super powerful microscope is that it is actually 99.999 percent empty space.[2] In fact, your hands, your body, and everything else that look and feel so real to you in this world are actually mostly empty space. This, of course, is not how you experience reality but science has made this remarkable discovery.

Now, we ask you to imagine turning the powerful telescope toward the heavens and the vastness of outer space. Scientists tell us that the universe is mostly empty space (although it also contains a vast amount of "dark matter" and "dark energy" neither of which is fully understood yet). Just as we perceive our physical world as real in spite of it being mostly empty space, what other realities are bypassing our perception?

For example, might we come to see, understand, and experience another proposed "invisible" phenomenon—the interconnectedness of all things, human, environmental, and beyond—in a way that feels as real as our hands feel to us today?

We don't know, but our only hope of uncovering new insights and new ways of understanding is to keep reconsidering so that we can continue to evolve into ever higher states of being and conscious awareness.

AFTERWORD

*"Our challenge today is to trust the power of
love at the heart of life, to let ourselves be seized
by love, to create and reinvent new ways for
love to evolve into a global wholeness of unity,
compassion, justice, and peacemaking."*

—ILIA DELIO

Constructing a map to the future using metaphors, stories,
and skill building is an imperfect methodology, but we
hope that you find in this book, at minimum, reasons
to be optimistic about the future. Even more so, we hope you are
captivated by a sense of human possibility and feel energized and
confident to develop your Re ideas, seeing yourself as a current
or future member of Generation Re, embracing a wholehearted,
personal commitment to building a regenerative future.

Acting on ideals that match the ethos of Generation Re will,
at times, feel like creating something out of nothing. But don't
despair. Creating something out of nothing is an age-old endeavor,
and all of our experiences have arisen out of the courage of our
ancestors to manifest their imaginations.

The following ancient folk paradox may offer some perspective: Which came first, the seed or the tree? It is a puzzling
question and one for which science provides a semisatisfying,
although incomplete, answer. Science says that trees came first.

The earliest trees used spores to procreate. In time, trees evolved the capability to produce seeds. This, however, begs a question: Did the spore or the tree come first? Again, science offers an incomplete answer, and we must keep reaching further down the rabbit hole in search of a complete answer until, ultimately, we reach the point where the final question becomes *How is something created out of nothing?*

This is where the limitless and inexhaustible powers of the human imagination come in. Is it possible that something else came before both the seed and the tree and that something else might endure long after them?

For consideration, we leave you with two powerful visuals. The first is the Celtic Tree of Life. It is an ancient symbol that reflects the holistic and interconnected nature of regeneration. In figure a.1, however, you will notice something different at the base of the tree, where the trunk and the roots diverge. It is a heart.

Figure a.1. The Celtic Tree of Life.

We leave it up to your imagination as to what the heart represents, but we encourage you to reflect deeply on the matter. Better yet, we encourage you to study this image from an artist named Seth, as you ponder the potent question of how you may sow seeds for a more regenerative future.

Figure a.2. A Seed So Quick to Take to the Soil.

NOTES

CHAPTER 1

1. Joseph Chilton Pearce, *The Biology of Transcendence: A Blueprint of the Human Spirit*, 2nd edition (Park Street Press, 2002).

2. Dev Tandon, *The OBO Premise: A Bold New Vision for Business* (self-pub., 2019), p. 32.

3. Sharyn Jackson, "Serving Sandwiches and Social Justice," *Minneapolis Star Tribune*, May 5, 2019.

4. Chris Lazlo and Judy Sorum Brown, eds., *Flourishing Enterprise: The New Spirit of Business* (Stanford Business Books, 2014), p. 10.

5. Terry Patten, *A New Republic of the Heart: An Ethos for Revolutionaries* (North Atlantic Books, 2008), p. 132.

6. Patten, *A New Republic of the Heart*, pp. 132–133.

7. Shannon Prather, "Gourmet Grilled Cheese Eatery Aims to Give Ex-Offenders a Second Chance," *The Atlanta Journal-Constitution*, February 15, 2018, https://www.ajc.com/lifestyles/food--cooking/gourmet-grilled-cheese-eatery-aims-give-offenders-second-chance/Wr1rZ3CABnVAbdb2yX3J6N/.

8. Theresa Bourke, "Spontaneous Pay-It-Forward Chain Lasts 2 Days, 900 Cars at a Minnesota Dairy Queen," *Alexandria Echo Press*, December 7, 2020.

9. Jules Evans, "Dissolving the Ego," *Aeon*, June 26, 2017.

10.   Parker Palmer, *The Courage to Teach* (John Wiley & Sons, 1997); Margaret Silf, *The Way of Wisdom* (Lion Books, 2006), p. 181.

11.   Ken Funk, "What Is a Worldview?," Oregon State University, https://web.engr.oregonstate.edu/~funkk/Personal/worldview.html.

12.   Alison J. Gray, "Worldviews," *International Psychiatry*, no. 3 (2011) 8: 58–60.

13.   David Whyte, *Just Beyond Yourself: The Courage in Poetry* (Many Rivers Press, 2018).

CHAPTER 2

1.   Elizabeth Chai Vasarhelyi, dir. *Free Solo. National Geographic*, 2018.

2.   "Interview: Let a Thousand Currencies Bloom—Bernard Lietaer," Great Transition Initiative, August 2017, https://greattransition.org/publication/let-a-thousand-currencies-bloom.

3.   "Credentials of a Flying Fish: Bernard's Story," Lietaer.com, https://www.lietaer.com/2021/01/credentials-of-a-flying-fish-bernards-story/.

4.   "Mission statement," Patagonia, https://mission-statement.com/patagonia/.

5.   Jim Geraghty, "A Billionaire Explains Why We Need Socialism," *National Review*, November 1, 2019, https://www.nationalreview.com/corner/a-billionaire-explains-why-we-need-socialism/.

6.   https://www.patagonia.com.au/pages/environmental-grants-and-support.

7.   Jeff Beer, "Patagonia Is in Business to Save Our Home Planet," *Fast Company*, December 13, 2018, https://www.fastcompany.com/90280950/exclusive-patagonia-is-in-business-to-save-our-home-planet.

8. Jeff Beer, "Patagonia CEO Rose Marcario Is Stepping Down," *Fast Company*, June 10, 2020, https://www.fastcompany.com/90515307/exclusive-patagonia-ceo-rose-marcario-is-stepping-down.

9. Beer, "'Patagonia Is in Business to Save Our Home Planet.'"

10. Douglas Bell, "How This Social Entrepreneur Turned $80 into a $43 Billion Housing Giant," *Forbes*, April 23, 2020, https://www.forbes.com/sites/douglasbell/2020/04/23/how-this-social-entrepreneur-turned-80-into-a-43-billion-housing-giant/?sh=37270e7a62bf.

11. "Our Story," Growing Greener Innovations, https://grengine.com/pages/our-story.

12. Olivia Goldhill, "Science Says Those Who Think They Are Experts Are More Likely to Be Closed-Minded," Quartz, November 1, 2015, https://qz.com/538308/science-says-those-who-think-they-are-experts-are-more-likely-to-be-closed-minded/.

13. Kamran Abbasi, "A Riot of Divergent Thinking," *Journal of the Royal Society of Medicine* 104, no. 10 (October 2011), https://www.ncbi.nlm.nih.gov/pmc/articles/PMC3184540/.

14. Reed Hastings, "How I Did It: Reed Hastings, Netflix," *Inc.*, https://www.inc.com/magazine/20051201/qa-hastings.html.

15. David Epstein, *Range: Why Generalists Triumph in a Specialized World* (Riverhead Books, 2019), p. 33.

16. Bogdan Draganski, Christian Gaser, Volker Busch, Gerhard Schuierer, Ulrich Bogdahn, and Arne May, "Changes in grey matter induced by training," *Nature*, 427, 311–312 (2004), doi.org/10.1038/427311a.

17. https://www.irva.org/speaker/mitchell-edgar.

CHAPTER 3

1. Elliott Katz, "When Hand-Washing Was Too Radical for Its Time," Aish, April 26, 2020, https://www.aish.com/ci/s/When-Hand-Washing-was-Too-Radical-for-its-Time.html.

2. Nina Strochlic, "'Wash Your Hands' Was Once Controversial Medical Advice," *National Geographic*, March 6, 2020, https://www.nationalgeographic.com/history/article/handwashing-once-controversial-medical-advice.

3. Logan Nye, "The Mathematician Who Saved Hundreds of Flight Crews," The Mighty, June 13, 2021, https://www.wearethemighty.com/popular/abraham-wald-survivor-bias-ww2/.

4. Sandee LaMotte, "Meet the Smoking-Free, Carbon-Negative Country That Passes No Law Unless It Improves Citizens' Well-Being," CNN, September 13, 2019, https://www.cnn.com/2019/09/13/health/bhutan-gross-national-happiness-.

5. LaMotte, "Meet the Smoking-Free, Carbon-Negative Country That Passes No Law Unless It Improves Citizens' Well-Being."

6. Justin McCarthy, "Happiness Is Not Quite As Widespread As Usual in the US," Gallup, January 10, 2020, https://news.gallup.com/poll/276503/happiness-not-quite-widespread-usual.aspx.

7. "Remarks at the University Of Kansas, March 18, 1968—Robert F. Kennedy," John F. Kennedy Presidential Library and Museum, https://www.jfklibrary.org/learn/about-jfk/the-kennedy-family/robert-f-kennedy/robert-f-kennedy-speeches/remarks-at-the-university-of-kansas-march-18-1968.

8. Business Roundtable, "Business Roundtable Redefines the Purpose of a Corporation to Promote 'An Economy That Serves All Americans,'" August 19, 2019, https://www.businessroundtable.org/business-roundtable-redefines-the-purpose-of-a-corporation-to-promote-an-economy-that-serves-all-americans.

9. "The Future of the Board of Directors," Harvard Law School Forum on Corporate Governance, https://corpgov.law.harvard.edu/2010/07/06/the-future-of-the-board-of-directors/.

10. "Larry Fink's 2020 Letter to CEOs: A Fundamental Reshaping of Finance," BlackRock, https://www.blackrock.com/us/individual/larry-fink-ceo-letter.

11. Klaus Schwab, "Davos Manifesto 2020: The Universal Purpose of a Company in the Fourth Industrial Revolution," World Economic Forum, December 2, 2019, https://www.weforum.org/agenda/2019/12/davos-manifesto-2020-the-universal-purpose-of-a-company-in-the-fourth-industrial-revolution/.

12. "Decarbonising Our Business," Unilever, https://www.unilever.com/planet-and-society/climate-action/decarbonising-our-business/.

13. Patrick Kennedy, "New C. H. Robinson Tool Will Help Companies Measure Their Carbon Footprints," *Star Tribune*, April 8, 2021.

14. Mary Meisenzahl, "Costco Is Raising Starting Wages to $17 an Hour," *Business Insider,* October 26, 2021, https://www.businessinsider.com/costco-raising-wages-to-17-an-hour-2021-10.

15. Hannah Baker, "Good Energy hiring teenagers to board in bid to tackle climate emergency," BusinessLive, November 27, 2020, https://www.business-live.co.uk/enterprise/good-energy-hiring-teenagers-board-19359860.

16. "11 Organic Organizations submit complaint to B Lab against Danone North America," Organic Farmers Association, https://organicfarmersassociation.org/news/blab/.

17. Public benefit corporations (PBC) and B Corps are different entities. PBC is a tax status, whereas B Corp is a certification for meeting the highest standards of concern for people, planet, and profit.

18. Centre for Public Impact, "Buurtzorg: Revolutionising Home Care in the Netherlands," November 15, 2018, https://www.centreforpublicimpact. org/case-study/buurtzorg-revolutionising-home-care-netherlands.

19. "Unilever Says No to 'Normal' with New Positive Beauty Vision," Unilever, August 3, 2021, https://www.unilever.com/news/press-and-media/press-releases/2021/unilever-says-no-to-normal-with-new-positive-beauty-vision/.

20. "Auto Repair Services," The Lift Garage, https://www.theliftgarage. org/wwd.

21. Thomas Kuhn, *The Structure of Scientific Revolutions* (University of Chicago Press), p. 158.

CHAPTER 4

1. "Greta Thunberg: 'I Don't Want Your Hope,'" *RealLeaders,* September 20, 2019, https://real-leaders.com/greta-thunberg-i-dont-want-your-hope/.

2. "Transcript: Greta Thunberg's Speech at the U.N. Climate Action Summit," NPR, September 23, 2019, https://www.npr. org/2019/09/23/763452863/transcript-greta-thunbergs-speech-at-the-u-n-climate-action-summit.

3. Christel Mesey, "Greta Thunberg's Speech to the World," Geneva Business News, December 21, 2018, https://www.gbnews.ch/greta-thunbergs-speech-to-the-world/.

4. Mark Kolakowski, "Amazon Launches $2 Billion Climate Venture Capital Fund," Investopedia, June 23, 2020, https://www.investopedia. com/amazon-launches-usd2-billion-climate-pledge-fund-5069567.

5. Umair Irfan, "Air Travel Is A Huge Contributor to Climate Change," Vox, November 30, 2019, https://www.vox.com/the-highlight/ 2019/7/25/8881364/greta-thunberg-climate-change-flying-airline.

6. Lloyd Alter, "'Flight Shaming' Is Really Reducing Short-Haul Flights in Europe,'" Treehugger, December 20, 2019, https://www.treehugger.com/flight-shaming-really-reducing-short-haul-flights-europe-4852960.

7. "History of Harvard Medical School," Harvard Medical School, https://mastersstudenthandbook.hms.harvard.edu/history-and-mission.

8. John Weeks, "Paradigm Shift? Harvard Medical School Considering Mission Reframe from Sickness to Health," *Today's Practitioner*, October 16, 2018, https://todayspractitioner.com/uncategorized/paradigm-shift-harvard-medical-school-considering-mission-reframe-from-sickness-model-to-health/#.YdYhzC9h0Xo.

9. Winston Churchill, "We Shall Fight on the Beaches," speech, June 4, 1940, America's National Churchill Museum, https://www.nationalchurchillmuseum.org/we-shall-fight-on-the-beaches.html.

10. "About Us," Tentree, https://www.tentree.com/pages/about.

11. Lola Akinmade Åkerström, "Why Are Swedes So Quiet?" *Slate*, September 20, 2013, https://slate.com/news-and-politics/2013/09/swedens-lagom-the-single-word-that-sums-up-the-swedish-psyche.html.

12. "The Clock of the Long Now," The Long Now Foundation, https://longnow.org/clock/.

13. "A Message from Co-Founder and CEO Brian Chesky," Airbnb News, May 5, 2020, https://news.airbnb.com/a-message-from-co-founder-and-ceo-brian-chesky/.

14. Matthew Fox, "Aboriginal Sense of the Sacred, continued," Daily Meditations with Matthew Fox, March 6, 2020, https://dailymeditationswithmatthewfox.org/2020/03/06/aboriginal-sense-of-the-sacred-continued/.

CHAPTER 5

1. Karen Cummings, "The Mystery of Starling Flight Patterns," *Cottage Life*, November 12, 2019, https://cottagelife.com/outdoors/the-mystery-of-starling-flight-patterns/.

2. Douglas W. Smith, Daniel R. Stahler, Matthew C. Metz, et al., "Wolf Restoration in Yellowstone: Reintroduction to Recovery," *Yellowstone Science* 24, no. 1, https://www.nps.gov/articles/wolf-restoration-in-yellowstone-reintroduction-to-recovery.htm.

3. "Sustainable Development Goal 1: End poverty in all its forms everywhere," United Nations, https://www.un.org/sustainabledevelopment/poverty/.

4. Kate Raworth, *Doughnut Economics: Seven Ways to Think Like a 21st-Century Economist* (Chelsea Green, London: Penguin Random House 2017).

5. Adele Peters, "Amsterdam Is Now Using the 'Doughnut' Model of Economics: What Does That Mean?" *Fast Company*, April 30, 2020, https://www.fastcompany.com/90497442/amsterdam-is-now-using-the-doughnut-model-of-economics-what-does-that-mean?position=1&campaign_date=04212021.

6. "Hamse Warfa Harnesses the Power of Blockchain to Help the World's Poorest Participate in the Global Economy with BanQu," Emerging Prairie, https://www.emergingprairie.com/hamse-warfa-harnesses-the-power-of-blockchain-to-help-the-worlds-poorest-participate-in-the-global-economy-with-banqu/.

7. Sonny Coloma, "Economy of Communion: Pathways to Inclusion," *Manila Bulletin*, June 17, 2021, https://mb.com.ph/2021/06/17/economy-of-communion-pathways-to-inclusion/.

8. Alan Jope, "The Unilever Compass," Unilever, November 5, 2020, https://www.unilever.com/news/news-search/2020/the-unilever-compass-our-next-game-changer-for-business/.

9. Jack Uldrich, "Unilever's 'Compass' Offers Other Companies a Sustainable Path to the Future," LinkedIn, March 2, 2021, https://www.linkedin.com/pulse/unilevers-compass-offers-other-companies-sustainable-path-uldrich/.

10. Bernard Marr, "The Amazing Ways How Unilever Uses Artificial Intelligence to Recruit & Train Thousands of Employees," *Forbes*, December 14, 2018, https://www.forbes.com/sites/bernardmarr/2018/12/14/the-amazing-ways-how-unilever-uses-artificial-intelligence-to-recruit-train-thousands-of-employees/?sh=7d137a776274.

11. Michael Blanding, "Best Buy: How Human Connection Helped Save a Failing Retailer," *Harvard Business Review*, May 4, 2021.

12. Blanding, "Best Buy: How Human Connection Helped Save a Failing Retailer."

13. Robert Booth, "Four-Day Week: Trial Finds Lower Stress and Increased Productivity," *The Guardian*, February 19, 2019, https://www.theguardian.com/money/2019/feb/19/four-day-week-trial-study-finds-lower-stress-but-no-cut-in-output.

14. Aziz Hasan, "Kickstarter CEO: Here's Why We're Trying Out a 4-Day Workweek," *Fast Company*, July 8, 2021, https://www.fastcompany.com/90653476/kickstarter-ceo-4-day-work-week.

15. Kristin Toussaint, "Hilary Cottam's 'Radical Help' Has Communities around the World Rethinking (and Revamping) Their Social Programs," *Fast Company*, August 4, 2020.

16. Alice Rawsthorn, "Hilary Cottam On Designing a Welfare State," *Wallpaper*, September 30, 2020.

17. Hilary Cottam, "Social Services Are Broken. How We Can Fix Them," TEDGlobal London, September 2015, https://www.ted.com/talks/hilary_cottam_social_services_are_broken_how_we_can_fix_them.

18. *The Dialogues of Plato*, trans. B. Jowette (Simon & Schuster, 1937), p. 316.

19. Samuel Bowles and Herbert Gintis, *A Cooperative Species: Human Reciprocity and Its Evolution* (Princeton University Press, 2013).

20. Ellie Anzilotti, "General Mills Has a Plan to Regenerate 1 Million Acres of Farmland," *Fast Company*, March 4, 2019, https://www.fastcompany.com/90313818/general-mills-has-a-plan-to-regenerate-1-million-acres-of-farmland.

21. "Cargill to Advance Regenerative Agriculture Practices across 10 Million Acres by 2030," *Successful Farming*, September 16, 2020, https://www.agriculture.com/cargill-to-advance-regenerative-agriculture-practices-across-10-million-acres-by-2030.

22. https://meaningful.business/team/alex-stephany/.

23. *The Circular Economy Show*, episode 1, "An Average Drill Is Only Used for 13 Minutes, How Does This Happen?" Ellen MacArthur Foundation, May 19, 2020, https://youtu.be/OegYcIDzu9o.

24. "The Luxury Curse Scam," *American Greed Podcast*, May 15, 2013, CNBC, https://www.cnbc.com/id/100738660.

25. http://www.humanagenda.net/tour-the-mondragon-cooperatives/.

26. P. E. Moskowitz, "Meet the Radical Workers' Cooperative Growing in the Heart of the Deep South," *The Nation*, April 24, 2017, https://www.thenation.com/article/archive/meet-the-radical-workers-cooperative-growing-in-the-heart-of-the-deep-south/.

27. Debi Roberson, Jules Davidoff, Ian R. L. Davies, and Laura R. Shapiro, "Colour Categories and Category Acquisition in Himba and English," in Nicola Pitchford and Carole P. Biggam, eds., *Progress in Colour Studies, vol. 2: Psychological Aspects* (John Benjamins, 2006), pp. 159–172.

28. John Koenig, *The Dictionary of Obscure Sorrows* (Simon & Schuster, 2021), p. 123.

29. Julia E. Hubbel, "How a Powerful Phrase from the Zulus Can Transform Our Relationships," *Medium*, March 30, 2020, https://medium.com/illumination/how-a-powerful-phrase-from -the-zulus-can-transform-our-relationships-6cce7bf1e63a.

30. Loom International, "Sawubona!" https://www.loominternational.org/ sawubona.

CHAPTER 6

1. Dennis Overbye, "A Tiny Particle's Wobble Could Upend the Known Laws of Physics," *New York Times*, April 11, 2021.

2. Ali Sundermier, "99.9999999% of Your Body Is Empty Space," *Business Insider*, September 23, 2016, https://www.businessinsider.com/physics- atoms-empty-space-2016-9.

PHOTO CREDITS

p. 117 figure 4.2.   Used under license from IStock, image credit: SeppFriedhuber Stockphoto ID:470062402

p. 131 figure 5.1.   Used under license from Shutterstock.com

p. 132 figure 5.2.   Image credit: Kate Raworth and Christian Guthier, CC-BY-SA 4.0

p. 132 figure 5.3.   Image credit: Kate Raworth and Christian Guthier, CC-BY-SA 4.0

p. 154 figure 5.5:   Used under license from Shutterstock.com

p. 162 figure 5.6:   Image credit: Fernando Losado Rodriguez. CC BY-SA 4.0, via Wikipedia Commons

p. 168 figure 5.7:   Image credit: https://gondwana-collection.com/blog/how -do-namibian-himbas-see-colour

p. 168 figure 5.8:   Image credit: https://gondwana-collection.com/blog/how -do-namibian-himbas-see-colour

p. 170 figure 5.9:   Image credit: David Novick, The University of Texas at El Paso, http://engineering.utep.edu/novick/colors/colorgifs/

p. 171 figure 5.10:   Image credit: David Novick, The University of Texas at El Paso, http://engineering.utep.edu/novick/colors/colorgifs/

p. 178 figure a.1:   Image credit: "Tree of Life," Greg McGee, St. Paul, MN

p. 179 figure a.2:   "A Seed So Quick to Take to the Soil" used with permission of Seth Pitt, artist

ABOUT THE AUTHORS

JACK ULDRICH is a leading global futurist, best-selling author of 14 books, member of the Forbes Business Council, a highly sought after keynote speaker, and poet. He makes regular appearances on major media outlets, including CNBC, NPR, and Fox. Uldrich is a former Naval Intelligence Officer and Defense Department official. He also served as the Director of the Office of Strategic Planning for the state of Minnesota. He lives in Minneapolis with his wife, Cindy. They have two children, Meghan and Sean. His outside interests include travel, hiking, reading, journaling, and pursuing matters of personal and spiritual growth. He and his wife will be taking a yearlong sabbatical in Ireland in 2023.

CAMILLE KOLLES, PhD, MPA, has been an executive in the nonprofit sector for nearly two decades and has served on the board of several local and national nonprofit organizations. She created national award-winning collaborations as a pioneer in the US movement to impact social change through the integration of classical performing arts and community development. Camille is currently an academic researcher of self-transcendence, inter-connectedness, and personal transformation, with recent research on social entrepreneurs. She received her PhD in Transformative Studies from the California Institute of Integral Studies and plans to launch The Center for Inspired Futures as an incubator for next-level thinking, connecting, and being. A classically trained pianist, she enjoys performing the occasional gig with her partner, Tim. Residing in Minneapolis, they enjoy Minnesota's gorgeous summers and the expanded awareness gained through travel.

www.ingramcontent.com/pod-product-compliance
Lightning Source LLC
Chambersburg PA
CBHW031851200326
41597CB00012B/363